KANSAS CITY'S PUBLIC LIBRARY

KANSAS CITY'S
PUBLIC LIBRARY

EMPOWERING THE COMMUNITY FOR
150 YEARS

JASON ROE

WITH CONTRIBUTIONS FROM MATT REEVES

Commemorating the 150th Anniversary of the Kansas City Public Library

Andrews McMeel Publishing
a division of Andrews McMeel Universal
1130 Walnut Street, Kansas City, Missouri 64106

www.andrewsmcmeel.com

24 25 26 27 28 VEP 10 9 8 7 6 5 4 3 2 1

ISBN: 978-1-5248-8809-1

Library of Congress Control Number: 2024933294

Editor: Jean Lucas
Art Director: Holly Swayne
Production Editor: Brianna Westervelt
Production Manager: Jeff Preuss

ATTENTION: SCHOOLS AND BUSINESSES

Andrews McMeel books are available at quantity discounts with bulk purchase
for educational, business, or sales promotional use. For information, please e-mail the
Andrews McMeel Publishing Special Sales Department: sales@amuniversal.com.

Dedicated to the patrons, staff, and supporters of the Kansas City Public Library

CONTENTS

MAYOR QUINTON LUCAS

Quinton Lucas, Mayor of Kansas City

I will never forget the day I received my library card in 1993. The old Main Library stood at Twelfth and McGee Streets downtown, perhaps lacking the charm and outward grandeur of today's Central Library. But my nine-year-old self was mesmerized. The Kansas City Public Library was my sanctuary. I was a child whose family moved often, and the Library was something I could always count on in most of our city's neighborhoods and, most importantly, was a place for me to grow.

The Library's books and periodicals taught me more than I could have ever imagined. I discovered our community's past, our heroes, our tragedies, our injustices, and I formed a lifelong love of our city in the old stacks at the Main Library location.

The Library's North-East, Waldo, and Lucile H. Bluford branches were all stops on my own tour of literary discovery and delight. From the Library's fixed locations to other, unassuming locations like the kiosk at the old Landing Shopping Center at Sixty-Third and Troost, I discovered that librarians had a simple mission: engaging with communities, wherever we were.

For the past 150 years, the Library has provided our neighborhoods with a welcoming, accessible, and equitable place to become informed and engaged community members. But Kansas City's library, like all public libraries, has become so much more today. It is leading attempts to bridge the digital divide; connecting residents with vital social services; providing access to health, education, and employment resources; and serving as a public forum and classroom for safe and impactful civil discourse. At the outset of the global COVID-19 pandemic, we saw our Library rise quickly and innovatively, leveraging strong relationships with local partners to continue to deliver an array of vital resources and services, and even expanding on them, to reach our community members.

The Kansas City Public Library is a source of great pride, for me and so many other community members. It continues to enrich and uplift our city and bring true, transformative change. Thank you to our librarians and all Library staff for being at the forefront of such great work.

Cheers to 150 years, and best wishes for many exciting new chapters.

A native of Kansas City, Quinton Lucas was elected as the city's fifty-fifth mayor in 2019.

PREFACE AND
ACKNOWLEDGMENTS

K ansas City's public library is the city's indispensable agent of community
empowerment. On its 150th anniversary, its continuity of purpose—and
its place at the heart of the city's civic culture—is clearer than ever. With a
history spanning three centuries, the Kansas City Public Library has been committed
to supporting patrons through literacy, intellectual freedom, and inclusion, each a
key component of a healthy democracy and thriving populace.

The following pages commemorate that venerable history and seek to understand
how the Library forged its modern identity during periods of accomplishment and
adversity. Rather than offering a strictly chronological account, chapters are organized
thematically to better convey the national and local trends that shaped the Library's
development. Service to children, outreach to the community, and engagement with
diverse communities are all important elements of the Library's history. Other chapters
recount historical episodes to explain the development of modern values in librarianship, showing how the Library's commitment to intellectual freedom expanded over
time. This is the story of a deep institutional relationship with the people of Kansas
City, and we hope this understanding of where the Library and city have been—the
triumphs and the challenges—will inform the system's many supporters as they
consider how it may best serve Kansas City in the future.

While researching and writing this book, we learned how beloved the Library
is to our community, a sentiment that stretches back further than living memory.
Besides reading thousands of pages of archival materials, published works, and media
coverage from the past 150 years, we also had the privilege of speaking with many
supporters, staff members, and civic leaders who enriched our understanding of
this vital institution. Special acknowledgments are given to Daniel Bradbury, Mary
Arney, Congressman Emanuel Cleaver II, Gloria Jackson-Leathers, Jonathan Kemper,
Crystal Faris, and Joel Jones for graciously sharing their Library experiences with us in

extended interviews, and to Mayor Quinton Lucas for sharing his personal experiences of the Library's community empowerment and support in action.

Our most important acknowledgment is to our Library patrons, the people of Kansas City, who have enabled the Library to serve this community for generations. Day-to-day points of contact—ordinary encounters numbering in the millions throughout its history—often escape the attention of media and the community at large. But, understood at scale, it is from these relationships that strong communities and vibrant democracies are built. Collectively, these routine experiences are no less important to the Library than the addition of a new branch or top-level organizational change. While appreciation abounds, the Library means something different to everyone, and we discovered through its patrons that its practices, its values, and the nature of its services to Kansas City have evolved tremendously over time.

Moreover, thousands of dedicated employees, leaders, and volunteers have tirelessly sustained the Library's success as a center of civic culture. The task of writing about such a treasured institution proved intimidating. It is our hope that we have been able to convey the importance of these numerous and diverse lived experiences, even though we could not possibly capture their sheer scale in a single book. It is you, the reader and Library supporter, who built the Library and will ensure its future.

During our work, we received research assistance from Cara Nordengren and Hannah Johnson—graduate students with Applied Humanities Fellowships through the Hall Center for the Humanities at the University of Kansas. They supplemented our research efforts; uncovered, organized, and prepared many of the book's images; participated in interviews; and served as helpful sounding boards at critical junctures. The staff of the Library's Missouri Valley Special Collections provided hundreds of primary and secondary source materials and images from the Library's rich archives and sifted through historical board minutes, microfilm, and other non-indexed materials.

Special thanks to Steve Wieberg, Anne Kniggendorf, John Herron, and Jeremy Drouin for their detailed proofreading and editorial insights. Finally, David LaCrone, Carrie Coogan, Joel Jones, Debbie Siragusa, and Pete Browne made this book possible by providing the time and support needed to consider the full depth of the Library's long and esteemed, if sometimes complicated, history.

—Jason Roe and Matt Reeves

INTRODUCTION

Any book that offered information on drawing was likely to be found listed on my card, and overdue books were the chief reason for my usually depleted bank account.

—WALT DISNEY

I n 1906, Elias Disney, the Canadian-born son of Irish immigrants, moved his young family from Chicago some four hundred miles southwest to a small farm near Marceline, Missouri. Disney had tried several careers, from railroad worker to professional fiddler, and in the early years of the century, he grew weary of the bustle of Chicago and hoped a rural setting would provide the family with more security and opportunity. Farming proved strenuous and financially fraught, and, as a result, the family relocated once again—this time to Kansas City in 1911. Urban life offered no respite from hard work, however. Elias and two of his sons performed several odd jobs, including newspaper delivery, rising each morning in the pre-dawn darkness, seven days a week, to make ends meet.

Despite the intense schedule, one of the boys, nine-year-old Walter, found a measure of tranquility in books. In the stories of Mark Twain, Horatio Alger, and Tom Swift, young Disney discovered worlds far removed from his rural Missouri setting. These books shaped what would become a remarkable life story, now best remembered for classic animated movies, theme parks, and, of course, a lovable cartoon caricature inspired by the mouse—according to one of several tales—that he kept in his Kansas City office, the Laugh-O-Gram animation studio.

In this noted American success story, the Kansas City Public Library played an unexpected and significant role. In 1937, the now world-famous Walt Disney, fresh off the success of his Academy Award–nominated *Snow White and the Seven Dwarfs*,

Newsboys outside *Kansas City Star* and *Times* offices in Olathe, Kansas, May 5, 1922

addressed a letter to the Library, expressing his appreciation for making his career possible. Library books had not just offered youthful escapism; they showed him his calling:

> *All during the early years of my youth, and a long time before I had given a career any thought, the Public Library has always held a tremendous interest for me. . . . Any book that offered information on drawing was likely to be found listed on my card, and overdue books were the chief reason for my usually depleted bank account. Later, in Kansas City, when I became seriously interested in cartooning, I gained my first information on animation from a book . . . which I procured from the Kansas City Public Library. I feel the Public Library has been a definite help for me all through my career.*

The Kansas City Public Library has long supported the ambitions of children and youth, especially those whose backgrounds resembled Disney's humble origins. An 1897 article in *The Kansas City Star* emphasized, "All children are invited to the children's room, from the boys and girls of the rich to the little newsboys on the streets: Indeed, the newsboys will receive special attention, for Mrs. Whitney has long been

Childhood home of Walt Disney, 3028 Bellefontaine Avenue, 1940

interested in getting them to come to the library and to take out books." *The Star* was referring to Carrie Westlake Whitney, the Library's first full-time director and, to this day, the only woman to hold the position permanently. The article also quoted Whitney directly: "We are after the boys in the streets. For several years we have been lending books to the newsboys and in all that time only one book has been lost. . . . If a boy or girl wants to come and write a composition, he may do so and books of reference will be brought out for his use."

Over the past 150 years, generations of patrons utilized the Kansas City Public Library for self-improvement, community enrichment, or as a safe space to exist without obligation or payment. Disney's letter implied an impact emblematic of the Library's highest aspirations of community service and cultural development. As Kansas City grew across the decades, the nature of these commitments expanded and changed, but the Library's mission remained constant. What started as a disparate collection of books supporting a small school district grew into a full-fledged cultural institution with the ambitious mission to bolster the people's welfare, inspire lifelong learning, and empower citizens through knowledge.

Over the years this empowerment took many forms. Just as Disney represents the arc of many who use the Library as a tool for personal improvement, other patrons

WALT DISNEY

August 17, 1937.

Miss Irene Gentry,
Acting Librarian,
Kansas City Public Library,
Kansas City, Mo.

Dear Miss Gentry:

Thank you for your letter of August 11. It gives me
pleasure to tell you how highly I regard the services
offered by the Public Libraries and especially that
of the Kansas City Library.

All during the early years of my youth, and a long time
before I had given a career any thought, the Public
Library has always held a tremendous interest for me.
Needless to say, any book that offered information on
drawing was likely to be found listed on my card, and
over-due books were the chief reason for my usually
depleted bank account.

Later, in Kansas City, when I became seriously interested in cartooning, I gained my first information on animation from a book written by H. C. Lutz which I procured from the Kansas City Public Library. I feel the
Public Library has been a very definite help to me all
through my career.

While we have established a sizeable library of our own,
nevertheless we are constantly calling upon the local
Public Library to supplement our needs from its vast
resources.

Mickey joins me in sending greetings to you and all the
members of the American Library Association.

Sincerely yours,

Walt Disney

WD:DV

Walt Disney's letter to Irene Gentry, Acting Librarian of the Kansas City Public Library, August 17, 1937

leverage Library resources for social change. If Disney helps us understand the mission of the young Library, few patrons embody the goals of the modern institution better than longtime human rights champion Alvin Sykes. Described by the *New York Times* as "the nation's most persistent advocate for civil rights-era justice," Sykes attained national acclaim despite a challenging childhood spent in foster care or boys' homes and suffering abuse at the hands of neighbors. He dropped out of school after the eighth grade and later quipped, "I transferred to the public library."

Sykes's life changed abruptly when his close friend, jazz musician Steve Harvey, who was Black, was murdered in Kansas City's Penn Valley Park on November 4, 1980. The talented Harvey, then twenty-seven, was killed by nineteen-year-old Raymond Bledsoe, who mistakenly believed that Harvey was gay because of the park's reputation as a meeting place for the city's gay community. At trial, Bledsoe was acquitted by an all-white jury despite testimony from two friends who aided in the assault. Outraged, Sykes called the US Department of Justice, only to learn that nothing could be done because of the Constitution's prohibition against double jeopardy.

Alvin Sykes with the Library's Executive Director R. Crosby Kemper III, standing in the reference section, Central Library

The undeterred Sykes, with assistance from Harvey's widow and an associate from the Justice Department's Community Relations Service, researched legal appeals at Kansas City's downtown Library. Sykes discovered that the Civil Rights Act of 1968 contained language that contradicted the Justice Department's reluctance to revisit the case. His activism prompted the Justice Department to reopen the case, and in 1983, Bledsoe was convicted of hate crimes and sentenced to life in prison for violating Harvey's civil rights.

Alvin Sykes standing at the entrance to the Central Library, ca. 2000s

From that point forward, and without a formal legal education, Sykes utilized the resources of the Kansas City Public Library to blaze a path as a self-described "human rights worker." His labors never earned him much money, but his activism resulted in national civil rights achievements. He worked with US Sen. Jim Talent (R-MO) to inaugurate the Emmett Till Unsolved Civil Rights Crime Act of 2008, a measure that passed in the US House with a 422–2 vote. His testimony before Congress and his lobbying efforts were widely credited with moving it through the Senate.

The bill, signed into law by President George W. Bush, authorized $13 million annually to reopen unresolved civil rights cases. In acknowledgment of his impact on racial justice, in 2013 the Library named Sykes its first "scholar in residence," a fitting post for someone who saw libraries as "the great equalizer."

"There was a time when somebody like me wouldn't have been allowed inside a library—or as a Black man permitted to read at all," Sykes said. "But I was able to revolve much of my life around the library. I sought and got my education there." In an obituary in the *New York Times*, Brian Levin, director of the California-based Center for the Study of Hate and Extremism, was effusive in his praise. "Anyone who worked in civil rights during the last several decades knew Alvin Sykes," Levin wrote. "He changed the face of American law, and he learned it all in a Kansas City library."

Over the past century and a half, the Kansas City Public Library has strengthened ties to its home city while embracing a common set of values: inclusion, access, privacy, diversity, intellectual freedom, and democracy. During this long history, the Library has been an agent for positive change, among other things serving as a national innovator in service to children and youth. It received the highest forms of national recognition and performed community engagement work that was much less heralded but no less important. The Library's value and promise to the patrons it serves was made crystal clear in 2018, when 83 percent of voters approved a property tax increase to support its continued growth and development.

This book explores that record of ambition, achievement, and, in some cases, historical shortcomings. The full spectrum of the Library's history is inseparable from that of Kansas City, which itself reflects the events and contested values that shaped this nation's legacy.

EARLY CHALLENGES

The Library's story begins in an untamed western town still recovering from the social and economic strife of the Civil War. Those who came to Kansas City to pursue personal opportunities spoke of a bright future for the city at large. Boosters, investors, and entrepreneurs aspired to build a great metropolis on the plains, quite apart from its wide-open-town reputation. However, lingering divisions and the side effects of unrestrained growth presented challenges for the city and, by extension, the fledgling Kansas City Public Library.

Less than a decade before the Library's establishment, the Civil War tore the nation apart. Deep political and racial divisions persisted even after its official conclusion, and as sharecropping replaced slavery, hopes of racial equality were dashed. Arguably no state was as divided by the war as Missouri, where a convention was called to consider secession in 1861. Missouri narrowly decided to remain in the Union, but as a slave state precariously positioned between North and South, it was in many ways like the nation—at war with itself. Conflicts that raged across the state's western border during the Bleeding Kansas era escalated into unsanctioned guerrilla warfare between Jayhawkers on the Union side and Bushwhackers on the Confederates'. In Kansas City, where secessionists briefly raised a Confederate flag at Second and Main Streets in spring 1861, it was unclear which sentiments would prevail.

Secessionists in Kansas City disavowed Mayor Robert Van Horn, a newspaper publisher who had been elected on a "moderate" platform that was Unionist but nonetheless pro-slavery. Missouri Gov. Claiborne Fox Jackson, a secessionist, tried to force Van Horn's resignation. Instead, Van Horn gained a Union commission and, in midsummer 1861, secured five companies of soldiers to set up "Camp Union" on the foundation of the still-unfinished Coates House Hotel at Tenth and Broadway, just a few blocks west of where the present-day Central Library would stand.

The war would soon come to Kansas City with a Confederate cavalry raid led by Maj. Gen. Sterling Price. The fighting culminated with the Battle of Westport in fall 1864. In the largest encounter west of the Mississippi River, Union forces repulsed the Confederates at Brush Creek, near the Library's current Plaza Branch. All told, Missouri experienced twelve hundred battles and skirmishes, more than any other state besides Virginia and Tennessee.

Even as the tensions and political issues of the Civil War cast a pall over the community, Kansas City experienced economic growth and a population boom. On July 3, 1869, four years before the Library's founding, the completion of the Hannibal Bridge situated the city as a major hub for railroad networks, trade, and commerce. Railroad commerce supplanted the era of steamboats, and Kansas City gained an economic edge over its regional rivals. The city's population—just over 4,000 in the 1860 census—exploded to more than 32,000 in 1870 and exceeded 165,000 by 1900. The Kansas City stockyards emerged as the second-largest livestock trade center in the world, and the city's booming garment industry, also the nation's second largest,

A reproduction of George Caleb Bingham's *Order No. 11*, depicting Union soldiers removing suspected Southern sympathizers from northwestern Missouri, is displayed behind the circulation desk of the Central Library

added to the economic foundation. Kansas City had it all—a major railroad network, a thriving business environment, and a populace eager for growth.

Its grand economic ambitions were confirmed at the Kansas City Industrial Exposition in September 1872, which attracted sixty thousand visitors a day, nearly double the city's population. Not unlike a world's fair, the event showcased state-of-the-art industrial machinery and cultural achievement. These expositions became an annual fixture of Kansas City culture over the next two decades, attracting politicians including President Grover Cleveland, as well as entrepreneurs and robber barons like Cornelius Vanderbilt.

Before Kansas City could claim its place as a cultured American metropolis, an unwelcome episode sullied the spectacle of the first exposition. Underscoring the city's persistent rough edges in 1872, the infamous Jesse and Frank James robbed the ticket booth in broad daylight. Despite stray gunfire that wounded a young girl, biographer T. J. Stiles describes how one local newspaper editor spun the narrative to portray the former-Confederate James brothers' criminal acts as heroic. Casting the outlaws as sympathetic protagonists who stole from the rich and opposed the postwar federal occupation of the South, the coverage crystallized the city's unique position in the national imagination.

These incidents and the many other unrefined elements of Kansas City were all too obvious at a time when reformers were trying to sell what the town could become. It is at this point that the Kansas City Public Library became part of the city's effort to remake itself. To those who imagined a great public library at the heart of a cultural outpost on the plains—a library worthy of the most cosmopolitan of American cities—it looked to be an uphill battle. An anonymous columnist in the city's primary newspaper, *The Kansas City Star*, put such views into print: "We have nothing to attract people here; nothing to keep them here when they chance to come, and our undesirable reputation in that regard has spread out over the entire country." The piece described Kansas City "as a place without a park or a drive; as a place with miles of unpaved . . . streets; as a city without a large free public library, and, finally, as a city that, having unequalled opportunities to be beautiful, chooses rather to remain unattractive and ugly."

The column in *The Star* confirmed what Library boosters knew all too well: If Kansas City was to transcend its roughshod roots and join the great cities of America,

Kansas City Public Library and school district offices at Eighth and Oak Streets, ca. 1889–1897

it needed public investment in parks and schools, businesses and museums, and perhaps above all else, a public library.

The Library was then part of the city's nascent school district and shared facilities with the district's offices. It had been founded December 5, 1873, but years would pass before the school board constructed its first purpose-built library building at Eighth and Oak Streets. Books could be checked out just one at a time and only then through a fee-based subscription service. The two-story brick structure—and the scope of service provided to Kansas City's energetic population—was far too modest for boosters who eyed Chicago and New York, not regional neighbors St. Joseph or Omaha, as worthy rivals. A stately public library would signal Kansas City's arrival as a great metropolis, as rich in culture as in cattle and textiles.

1

LIBRARY PROSPECTING IN A WILD WESTERN TOWN

A fountain of intelligence and refinement, whose pure waters will flow into the palace of the rich and the cottage of the poor, bringing health, prosperity and happiness. It can be relied upon that this library is permanent, and much may be expected from it.

—J. V. C. KARNES, KANSAS CITY SCHOOL BOARD PRESIDENT

From its founding, the Kansas City Public Library supported the cultural aspirations of its hometown, a rugged city situated at America's crossroads. The Library's early promoters linked their efforts with those of city boosters who saw it as part of an initiative to heal the divisions of the Civil War, transcend the city's "cowtown" roots, and push the community toward a culturally refined future. In 1882, school board president Robert L. Yeager made an even bolder statement about the Library's importance: "We believe that if the public could be made to realize that a magnificent library adds largely to the material growth of a city . . . we would

Main Street in Kansas City, Missouri, looking north from Sixth Street, 1870

soon have a 'boom' on the library that would astonish us all. May the 'boom fever'
strike the library."

Despite such lofty goals, the Library had modest origins. When its doors first
opened, it consisted of little more than a school board resolution and unrealized
plans for a small book collection. Library proponents faced considerable headwinds
in a divided community, made worse by an international economic depression. A
fiscal crisis swept the United States, lasting through much of the 1870s, and in this
context the early Library could expect only limited resources. Indeed, the city's first
public school "library" consisted of a single bookcase, purchased from Col. William
E. Sheffield, and a handful of random books. The bookcase, sometimes referred to as
the "Sheffield bookcase," is still in the Central Library today.

To raise money for a more substantial collection, the school district began hosting
public lectures, a Library tradition that endures to this day. St. Louis native Phoebe
Couzens, a noted suffragette and Missouri's first female law school graduate, delivered the inaugural lecture. The school board intended the lectures to do more than

raise resources. These events positioned the Library as the city's leader in educational and cultural affairs while improving civic pride and boosting interest in Kansas City. The lecture series, one contemporary observer noted, was unmatched in the region: "No superior entertainment has ever been offered to our people."

On December 5, 1873, the Kansas City Board of Education passed the following resolution:

Resolved. That there be established in connection with our schools a library for the use of the officers, teachers and scholars of the public schools of this district, to be known as the Public Library of Kansas City. Resolved. That an annual appropriation be made of such sums as the Board of Education may deem expedient, to be used exclusively as a library fund, . . . Resolved. That there be a standing committee on the library who shall be charged with the management and control thereof, subject to the supervision of this board.

These early outreach efforts were especially successful with the city's women's organizations. One, the Ladies' Centennial Association, a group connected to the legacy of the American Revolution, donated $490 in 1874 (equivalent to a little more than $13,000 today). Combined with modest income from the lectures, it gave the Library enough resources to purchase more than one hundred books, including an incomplete set of the *American Encyclopedia*. One hundred books hardly constituted a grand collection, but it was on this foundation that the Kansas City Public Library took shape.

In 1874, the Kansas City school board appointed James M. Greenwood as superintendent of schools and director of the Library. In December of the same year, the small library moved with the school board from the high school at Eleventh and Locust Streets to Greenwood's new office in the Sage Building at Eighth and Main Streets. The books had been available for reference, not lending, but starting in November 1876, Greenwood made the fledgling collection of more than one thousand books available for circulation. The Library was now "public"—not free but accessible through a subscription service that allowed patrons, for two dollars a year, to check out one book at a time. Subscribers could visit the space during a brief window on

Saturday afternoons. The Library moved again in 1879, into the Piper Building at 546 Main Street, and, for the first time, added subscriptions to periodicals, several of which are still in its catalog a century and a half later.

The works in this collection gave Kansas City residents access to a shared cultural dialogue that Greenwood himself had longed for as a child. Born in Illinois in 1837, he moved with his family to Adair County, Missouri, in 1852. The closest school was seven miles away, and its meager supply of textbooks could not satisfy his reading appetite. The enterprising young man resorted to selling a family steer to raise money to buy classical literature, Latin- and Spanish-language works, and books on algebra, geometry, surveying, and philosophy. He attended the Methodist seminary in Canton, Missouri, in 1857 and read law with his uncles.

Greenwood started teaching, married Amanda McDaniel in 1859, and served in the Union's Missouri State Militia between 1861 and 1864. After leaving the military, he taught in Lima, Illinois; Kirksville, Missouri; and eventually at Mount Pleasant College in Huntsville, Missouri. In June 1874, Kansas City's Board of Education invited him to lead the school district as superintendent. During the forty-year tenure that ensued, Greenwood oversaw incredible growth in the system, higher attendance, and implementation of the earliest high school programs in laboratory science and literature in the West.

His dual roles as superintendent and Library director underscored the Kansas City Public Library's lineage to the city's school district. The school system dated to 1866 and the conclusion of the Civil War. Its formation was not without controversy, having arisen through a series of state laws, the "Parker Laws," which were passed in 1865 to establish compulsory taxation for public education. These statutes were drafted by anti-Confederate "Radical Republicans" who were hardliners on qualifications for the readmission of seceded states and who were insistent on loyalty oaths from suspected Southern sympathizers. Pro-Confederates, by contrast, opposed any Reconstruction-era education laws that contributed to the social and economic advancement of African American students and communities. Additionally, public education came with a historical class-based stigma as a program for the poor, lessening its appeal as a universal public good. Private schools were widely considered the gold standard.

Navigating the divisions of the time, Kansas City created the public school district, elected its first school board, and held classes for the first time in rented rooms

The Kansas City Public Library's original bookcase on display at the Main Library, 1897

and church basements in 1867. By 1872, about four thousand students (out of the city's six thousand school-age children of all races) attended school in nine dedicated buildings: Washington, Humboldt, Franklin, Benton, Lathrop, Morse, Woodland, Lincoln (the city's only elementary school available to Black students), and Central (the high school for white students only). Lincoln High School opened at Nineteenth and Tracy Avenue in 1890, making secondary education more widely available to Black students on a segregated basis.

AMERICA'S PUBLIC LIBRARY: "A LIBRARY OF THE CHOICEST BOOKS"

The expansion of Kansas City's public schools was matched by a growing library, and both were part of a nationwide education boom. The modern version of public libraries as book-lending institutions supported by community taxes had not arrived in the United States until the mid-nineteenth century. Prior to that, citizens did not have free and open access to information, reference works, great literature, or other published cultural capital. Public libraries, including the small system in Kansas City, were seen as a much-needed corrective, democratizing access to information. It is true that this noble philosophy came with an elitist tinge—few looked to libraries to provide frivolous entertainment or "tawdry" fiction. Rather, they began multiplying across the nation as sources of civic uplift.

The movement took cues from the handful of private lending libraries that existed in the eighteenth century. Sometimes called "social libraries," they were modeled on Benjamin Franklin's 1732 Library Company of Philadelphia, which housed books that tradesmen could use for professional development, or "useful knowledge." Franklin also joined many of his colonial colleagues in purchasing books that they would collectively own and share. He encouraged book discussion groups, often held in rented rooms in taverns and almost always lubricated with wine, as part of a growing intellectual culture in the young American republic.

Through a private subscription model, the Library Company of Philadelphia and other like-minded social libraries expanded book access to a wide cross-section of subscribers. More than fifty such libraries dotted colonial New England, and these institutions became embroiled in the political debates of the age. Works by Thomas Jefferson, John Locke, Samuel Adams, and many others could be found in their collections, and the ideas discussed in social libraries helped fuel the revolutionary movement.

The American social library had a decidedly political bent, but its companion institution—the private circulating library—was more populist, activist, and market-driven. Spreading throughout the late colonial era, circulating libraries also allowed patrons to access books for a fee. Membership included fewer social elites, however, appealing directly to broader audiences. Often, the most-circulated reading materials were not philosophical works but romances, murder stories, and other popular fiction.

Although advocates for the classics scoffed, popular fiction created an American literary culture that fueled support for public libraries in communities across the continent. In the opening decades of the nineteenth century, the rapid rotary press lowered printing costs, bringing a shift in reading habits from the intensive and repetitive reading of a few expensive texts to more diverse audiences poring through plentiful and affordable books. Breadth of reading displaced depth, and widespread demand for fiction was confirmed when public libraries gained a footing in the second half of the nineteenth century.

Social libraries proudly supported an informed citizenry and the advancement of democracy, yet their fee-based services and concept of democracy usually extended only to the middle- or upper-class white (and often male) citizens who mirrored the libraries' leadership. In the early nineteenth century, women were not allowed in many prominent libraries, and collections policies often restricted women's access to books believed to contain "corrupt" moral themes. African Americans encountered even harsher proscriptions against literacy and education. In slaveholding Missouri, for instance, teaching Black people to read had once been a criminal offense, and accessing books remained a challenge for many individuals on society's edges.

As the number of social and circulating libraries expanded in the nineteenth century, barriers to access continued. It would fall to another sort of library, the public library, to utilize community resources and reach out to a more diverse audience. In 1835, the state of New York established the first school district libraries accessible to the public, then went on to accumulate 1.5 million books over the next fifteen years. By 1851, the Boston Public Library not only allowed anyone access to its collections but also obtained numerous copies of the most popular books of the time, all to encourage a shared literary culture in the community.

Despite inching toward wider access, many public libraries still tightly controlled their collections. Patrons could not browse the stacks, and limited hours of operation, subscriptions, or other fees discouraged working-class borrowers. Some public libraries banned works of fiction from their collections or, as in Chicago, restricted the number of copies of popular fiction to discourage readers from embracing the genre. Even the comparatively progressive Boston Public Library censored women's access to certain books. In Kansas City, however, the public library bucked national trends and became a beacon for community cultural engagement, thanks to the efforts of a dynamic director.

CARRIE WESTLAKE WHITNEY: MOTHER OF THE KANSAS CITY PUBLIC LIBRARY

The Kansas City Public Library's distinctive early development was forged by Carrie Westlake Whitney, the first full-time head librarian for the system and its manager through a period of tremendous growth. Her innovations included free book lending to the public, an enhanced commitment to children's literacy, engagement with professional library organizations nationwide, and investment in two notable civic institutions: the Nelson-Atkins Museum of Art and the Kansas City Museum.

Whitney appeared abruptly on Kansas City's public scene, so it is fitting that many aspects of her life remain enigmatic more than a century later. Every biographical account, each census after 1880, and her death certificate state that she was born in 1854 in Fayette County, Virginia. Her southern roots are certain, and she once described her family as "southern people," but her age is less clear, as different records and her own accounting offer discordant birth years. We know that she was born Caroline E. Westlake, to farmers Wellington Westlake and Hellen Van Waters, and had at least three siblings.

Carrie Westlake Whitney, head librarian, 1881–1910

Sometime before 1856, the Westlakes moved to Iowa to live near relatives. Civil War draft records from 1863 suggest that the family was still living in the same county, but after Carrie's mother passed away sometime around 1868, her father moved near Sedalia, Missouri, to live with extended family. Around the same time, Carrie resided with her uncle in St. Louis and attended local schools. Little else is known about her education, but she read widely and would become a respected author in later years.

Thanks to marriage records, we can place Whitney in Sedalia in 1875, when she married Dr. Edward W. Judson. He had been a student at the Polytechnic Institute of Washington University in St. Louis in 1871, which overlapped with Whitney's time attending school in the same city. Within a few years of their marriage, however, they separated. When Carrie moved to Kansas City, she still went by the name Carrie W. Judson, but she was on her own, and Edward was living in St. Louis. Census records from 1880 show that she worked as a bookkeeper and was boarding with none other than school superintendent James Greenwood and his family.

At the time that Whitney took charge of the Library in 1881, the collection, which was housed in the cramped school board offices at 546 Main Street, consisted of two thousand books plus a handful of government records and periodicals. Book lending took place on a subscription basis, and just one small reading room opened to the public in the late evenings. At the near-exact moment of Whitney's arrival in the city, an editorial in *The Star* encouraged civic leaders to strengthen cultural institutions like the public library. "The advantages to be derived from such an institution can hardly be estimated," it said. "It will be a moral agent more powerful than a church and will at once solve the difficult question, 'What amusement shall we furnish to the young stranger within our gates?'"

The article continued, "At present it is alarming to consider the temptations which beset the incoming youth. He finds no public library, no regular place of amusement except variety halls and saloons where he can meet congenial companions and in consequence he goes astray." Whitney undoubtedly agreed and set out to offer the Kansas City Public Library as a corrective.

Working with the school board, she campaigned to expand the Library's reach and, in the process, improve the lives of Kansas City youth. Board president J. V. C. Karnes supported her vision with a bold plan: "a large circulating library with [a] reading room, art galleries, and the like—a fountain of intelligence and refinement, whose pure waters will flow into the palace of the rich and the cottage of the poor,

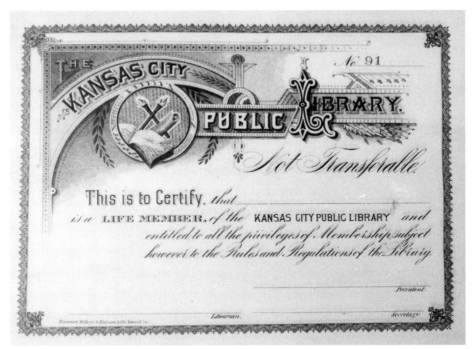

Subscription coupon for life membership to the Kansas City Public Library

bringing health, prosperity and happiness." Said Karnes, "It can be relied upon that this library is permanent, and much may be expected from it."

Whitney initially pursued goals of a practical nature. She set out to secure a proper and "more commodious" reading room, increase the number of subscribers to generate more annual revenue, and acquire "the best books." In all of this, she expressed a special interest in shaping the Library to cater to the needs of children: "Every quality that man or woman has is incipient in the child and needs development and exercise." Years later, in an autobiographical sketch, she considered her greatest achievement to be "her influence with children."

Whitney had grand hopes, to be sure, but financial realities and the legal entanglements of Missouri politics conspired to stunt the Library's growth. State laws did not permit general tax revenues to fund public libraries, limiting the budget in Kansas City to subscriptions, fundraisers, and private donations of books and money. Creative solutions included the school board asking J. W. Perkins, principal of the Washington School, to devote his summer vacation in 1881 to seeking book donations house-to-house, on a wagon hired just for the purpose. Such grassroots efforts were piecemeal at best, but in 1883 the Missouri General Assembly allowed cities to appropriate $2,500 annually to libraries. With its first stable budget, the Kansas City Public Library moved in 1884 to a larger space on the northeast corner of Eighth and Walnut Streets, a couple of blocks from the current Central Library.

As Whitney's professional ambitions paid dividends, significant developments occurred in her personal life. In 1885, she married James Steele Whitney, a reporter for *The Kansas City Star* and former editor of *The Democrat*, a newspaper in Dayton, Ohio. School district guidelines precluded the employment of married female teachers (a restriction that remained in place until a teacher shortage during World War II), but the policy did not extend to the Library, and Whitney remained firmly in charge after her nuptials. That same year, the school board's president, Robert Yeager, expressed confidence in her leadership, proclaiming her "the right person in the right place. Kind, patient, firm and intelligent, she has the good-will of the patrons, and she is entirely competent to assist those who desire information as to a proper course of reading."

Little is known about James Whitney, but like his new bride, he does not appear to have adhered closely to tradition. He came to Kansas City in 1884 and was only twenty-one when he married Carrie, who was at least thirty-one (and more likely thirty-four). Even friends were surprised by their nuptials. His byline soon disappeared from *The Star*, and just a year after their marriage he briefly entered the printing business, then later went into real estate. However, James "broke down," according to an obituary, and moved to Denver. Suffering from tuberculosis and following medical advice of the time, he moved to the drier climate of Colorado to live with Carrie's brother and sister. He died in 1890, and to acknowledge the loss, the Library closed for a day preceding his burial in Elmwood Cemetery. The twice-wed Carrie, now nearly forty, retained the Whitney name and never married again. From then on, the Kansas City Public Library came first.

Her dedication was evident in her efforts to expand children's book "deposits" or "substations," which were shelves in school offices where children and teachers could collect their books placed on hold. These substations had cropped up in several of the city's elementary schools by 1885. Though committed to expanding access to books and literacy, Whitney remained skeptical of popular fiction and denounced "the national taste for reading trashy literature." She favored reading that stimulated thought, whereas "sensational literature is addressed to the feelings, and this is chiefly the reason why it perverts the taste and darkens the judgement." During her second year as librarian, she took solace in circulation statistics showing that in Kansas City, fiction accounted for less than half of all book circulation, far below the national average.

Whitney believed that children needed guidance as they developed individual reading tastes. She grew concerned about the reliance on standardized textbooks and complained that "much of the supplementary reading in the schools is only worth a place in the waste basket." As a solution, she said, "It is the duty of the Librarian to cultivate a taste for good reading in the mind of the reader, where the habit has not been formed, and then to guide it into the channels of intelligent research, or at least to point the way to the best thoughts that have been written by the greatest minds of all ages. In this way the library becomes a great educational center, whose influence in a community cannot be estimated."

Whitney's philosophy influenced reading pedagogy across the district as she pushed teachers to read children's books themselves and use their lessons to cultivate a love of reading among the city's youth. Light fiction such as *The Adventures of Tom Sawyer* or *Twenty Thousand Leagues Under the Sea* could be introduced, if necessary, to get children interested in reading. After gaining a child's trust, librarians were to move to more serious literature. Or, in Whitney's more colorful description, "begin by lifting a veal cutlet and in time you can lift a cow."

Whitney was a pioneer in public library practice, and her commitment to service and innovation resulted in constant growth. The Library relocated again in September 1889 to Eighth and Oak Streets, inside a two-story brick building constructed for the then-princely sum of $10,000. The project was only possible because of another amendment to state law that allowed school districts to erect structures specifically for library use. The Library filled the entire first floor and now consisted of fifteen thousand volumes, a large reading room, and a stenographer's room. Private reading clubs had flourished over the previous decade, and they utilized the Library's growing collections and meeting spaces. A dedicated chess and checkers room was considered a unique innovation, intended to eliminate the disruptions of those games being played in the old reading room. Subscriptions to newspapers across the country connected Kansas City readers with national news on an unprecedented scale.

The new Library was an architectural gem, with a combination of traditional gas and newfangled electric chandeliers providing artificial illumination. But even those creature comforts did not alter seasonal reading habits. "There is comparatively little reading in summer and it is all in the lighter vein," Whitney said, noting that "high temperature is not at all conducive to the headwork necessary in reading heavy literature." She was pleased to note, however, that in winter, next to cozy fireplaces, the public read prolifically about art, poetry, French language and literature, philosophy, theology, history, and science. "I know of no city where history is given as much attention as here," she told *The Kansas City Times*. "This is due, probably, to the fact that a number of classes in history are organized here every winter."

Whitney also reassured the *Times*'s reporter: "No trashy fiction can be found on our shelves; we have even excluded the stories of Mrs. Amelie Rives-Chanler." Rives-Chanler's first novel, *The Quick or the Dead?*, had been published the year before and explored a widowed woman's struggle with erotic desire. Deemed by critics to be "immoral" and "unfit to be read," it nonetheless sold three hundred thousand copies. Kansas Citians interested in that title would have to purchase their own copies.

Innovation continued as a budget increase in 1892 freed Whitney to "experiment," as she described it, in permitting high school students to check out books without paying for subscriptions. The following year, she extended the benefit to sixth and seventh graders. Whitney continued to question students' reading habits, and the Library introduced a "pay collection" of popular fiction titles. The experience proved successful in increasing circulation. The Library eliminated paid subscriptions for all city residents in 1898.

When Whitney opened the new downtown Library, *The Kansas City Times* declared it a "permanent . . . commodious and well-arranged building." But despite its numerous advances, a visit there might not have enhanced the cultural enrichment of the average Kansas Citian. The Library still mirrored the paradox of Kansas City as an emerging urban center with modern ambitions but plenty of rough edges. Patrons came in by foot, horse, or trolley car, their boots carrying mud and manure from unpaved streets.

One long-serving librarian described the Library of the 1890s as follows:

Just imagine a street filled with old time-worn wagons—a dearth of human effects and with the usual bevy of children who were propelled maybe in their modest way by a team of oxen or maybe a span of worn-out horses. But we had street cars drawn by horses along the line of transportation on the Troost Cars. At this time our library was not a free public library but a place to send old time-worn books and magazines. . . . Our Reading Room was a comfortable place to spend an hour or two whenever the doors were open.

EMERGENCE AT LOCUST STREET

That frontier library experience improved dramatically in the fall of 1897, when patrons in Kansas City could finally visit a facility appropriately sized for a booming city of 150,000 people. A classical, Second Renaissance Revival–style building opened at Ninth and Locust Streets after three years of construction, costing $200,000. The marble facade above the main entrance read "Public Library" and was flanked by a pair of limestone pedestals topped by Ionic columns of marble with iron and bronze lanterns. Guests entered a large rotunda through golden oak doors with beveled glass. Said one librarian upon the building's opening, "This is the day when we open our arms and embrace the world."

The rotunda made a striking impression. Terrazzo floors were accented by bands of red and white ceramic tile in geometric patterns, and grey and yellow marble graced the wainscoted walls. Ornate columns with matching pilasters supported the ceiling, which was decorated with frescoes of angels, cupids, birds, ribbons, and roses, set against a background of clouds painted by Jerome Fedeli, a foreign consul from Italy. The main public service desk, located at the north end of the rotunda, was similarly crafted from marble. Behind the counter sat two large stained-glass windows depicting poets Henry Wadsworth Longfellow and William Cullen Bryant, fabricated by the local Campbell Paint and Glass Company.

The last noteworthy feature was a large fireplace, framed by a mosaic of soft rust-brown tesserae and colonnettes of black Egyptian marble with their own frieze of yellow marble veined in brown. Smaller fireplaces adorned most of the other rooms as well. The Renaissance Revival design echoed national library trends and was reminiscent of the Boston Public Library, completed several years earlier. With several extensive remodeling projects and an expansion in 1917–18 that doubled its size to more than sixty thousand square feet, the building would serve as the Main Library until 1960.

Top: Main Library building, looking northeast, Ninth and Locust Streets
Bottom: Main reading room, 1897

As Whitney correctly understood, the new library building unlocked cultural possibilities. The people of Kansas City finally possessed a free and open community space with fully equipped reading areas, browsing stacks, a newspaper reading room, and a large art gallery lit by a majestic skylight on the second floor, as well as a science museum on the ground floor. There was even a state-of-the-art ventilation system that supplied both heated and cooled air and a modern bindery department enabling on-site book repairs.

Fireplace and rotunda, 1897. The inscription above the fireplace reads, "There is nothing that solidifies and strengthens a nation like reading of the nation's own history, whether that history is recorded in books or embodied in customs, institutions, and monuments."

Into this grand palace of enlightenment, Whitney added a dedicated children's department catering to young readers' unique needs, including the provision of kid-size chairs and tables. It was, at the time, believed to be one of the first resources of its kind in any library in the United States. A "ladies' club room" on the second floor provided space for the meetings of Kansas City's numerous women's suffragist, temperance, and social clubs, as well as a spacious lecture hall that could hold literary and speaking events.

The new facilities were so avant-garde that they disqualified Kansas City from receiving funding from Andrew Carnegie. In 1899, the famous captain of the steel industry launched his first major wave of philanthropy, resulting in the construction of more than sixteen hundred public libraries across the United States. Grants were reserved for library buildings in communities that lacked adequate facilities, and Kansas City had already sped ahead of the curve. An editorial in *The Star* did not bemoan the loss of Carnegie support, opining that modern, progressive cities should fund their own libraries as "monuments to their own public spirit, generosity and intelligence."

The new Library's grand opening spanned two days, and Whitney welcomed twenty thousand visitors to soak up an atmosphere of palms, sunflowers, potted plants, and orchestral music. High school students ushered guests around the majestic building. It was an auspicious moment, and still more growth awaited.

In 1894, George Sheidley, a carriage maker turned real estate developer, had given the Library $25,000, the first large donation in its history. This massive gift (the equivalent of $800,000 in 2024) allowed the Library to expand its collection by nearly a third (to forty thousand volumes), adding important titles in art, reference, and language arts. James Greenwood soon donated three hundred additional books on arithmetic, creating one of the most comprehensive collections on math in the nation. In March 1898, the Library bolstered its holdings by acquiring the Jackson County Medical Library and making it available to area physicians.

By the turn of the century, the Library staff consisted of Whitney, an assistant librarian, ten library assistants, eight library pages, and three Sunday assistants. The bindery department employed a supervisor and four assistants. Three janitors and an engineer maintained the building. In a short span, Whitney had transformed the Kansas City Public Library into one of the most distinctive public libraries in the country. That she was able to accomplish so much in a brief time was not without

Top: Children's room with young readers, ca. 1900
Bottom: Rotunda and delivery desk, Kansas City Public Library at Ninth and Locust Streets, 1897

controversy or struggle, but there is little doubt that as the community looked forward, the city's public library stood as a crown jewel.

PROFESSIONAL WOMEN IN A MAN'S WORLD

Whitney cultivated a stern image to reinforce her professional standing in a time when women's opportunities were limited, but her management style struck a balance in support of her staff. Amid the formal, opulent atmosphere of the Main Library, visitors would have seen library pages, all high school boys, flitting about in green and gold uniforms as they reshelved books—and occasionally engaged in pranks.

One evening, Whitney saw a line of boys at a window on the second floor; they were climbing outside and sliding down a telephone pole. Whitney later explained where the idea originated: "I had given orders that no boy should leave the building by way of the steps." Taking the directive too literally, one of the older youths reasoned that the telephone pole was a viable alternative. In another publicized incident, a page swung a dead cat from a balcony and smacked a school district official in the face. Whitney intervened to save the boy's job. She later reported that he graduated from a large college in the East and that many of the other ornery boys had matured and found success in libraries and beyond.

A more serious matter developed just after dark on February 8, 1898, when Whitney and the assistant librarian, Frances A. Bishop, were leaving work. At the corner of Eighth and Locust, a drunk man "staggered toward them from the shadow across the street" and, according to *The Star*, followed and called out to them as they retreated toward the Library. The two women eventually found refuge with a couple walking nearby. Whitney asked the city council to keep a lamp lit at the intersection, and she requested permission from the police commissioners to carry a revolver for self-defense.

A newspaper account of the incident marks one of the first references to Frances Bishop, who was Whitney's likely romantic partner for roughly forty years. City directories indicate that almost every year, Whitney moved from one apartment or boarding arrangement to another between 1885 and 1916, with Bishop accompanying her throughout the latter half of those years. These residences were never more than a short walk from the Main Library. On the night that Bishop and Whitney were frightened, they had planned to take a streetcar from the Library to their residence near the intersection of Tenth Street and Broadway. Bishop followed closely in Whitney's footsteps as a woman finding professional accomplishment in one of the few fields in which that was possible at the time.

Whitney transformed the public library in Kansas City, but she was also active in the larger movement for professionalization in the field. This effort, just gaining steam across the country, brought both opportunities and limitations for women like her. Kansas City gave Whitney the unusual prospect of guiding an important civic organization from infancy to its establishment as an enduring institution with dozens of employees. Yet she also faced social and economic hurdles; her starting salary in 1881, for example, was just thirty dollars per month, less than half of what was paid to local female teachers.

For the founding generation of the library profession, women's involvement and lower pay was intentional. The nation's first library school opened at Columbia University in 1886, founded by Melville Dewey, eponymous with the cataloguing system in widespread use today. Defying the college's moratorium against female students, Dewey admitted seventeen women to the first class of twenty. He viewed librarianship as part of the women's sphere, aligned with the accepted social role for women in education for future generations of civically engaged readers. Dewey likewise reasoned that librarianship would not compete with established male professions and that the lower pay scale for women would further his goal of providing service to "the greatest number at the least cost." Dewey's views influenced the establishment of the American Library Association (ALA), and in the early twentieth century, women constituted more than 70 percent of library staff nationwide.

Even as patrons, women received mixed treatment at libraries. Some public libraries separated the sexes at different tables, which chafed the attendants responsible for separating spouses who wanted to sit together. The Kansas City Public Library did not impose such restrictions, but librarians did attempt to direct the reading habits of women and girls toward traditionally feminine literature. Even innocuous reforms could bring unintended consequences. The unrestricted browsing of shelves, for example, generated complaints in a New Jersey library when women—wearing the restrictive clothing of the time—had difficulty kneeling to access lower bookshelves or could not climb the sliding ladders that leaned against bookcases. Similar issues arose locally. *The Kansas City Times* reported in 1890 that "(a) young woman reading a periodical at one of the tables had her left leg accidentally (?) exposed so that a pink stocking was visible up to her knee. She was quietly asked to leave."

Whitney joined this national conversation, augmenting her reputation as the force behind the Kansas City Public Library. She organized and supported university extension classes as early as 1891, a marked achievement for any public library. Whitney served on the Chicago World's Fair (officially the World's Columbian Exposition) educational commission in 1893, was pictured in a *Bookman of New York* article about prominent women working in libraries in 1897, and secured braille books for use by blind patrons in 1898. In 1900, she began a monthly library bulletin and distributed it throughout the community to publicize new books, policies, and events.

Whitney also emerged as a regular public speaker, especially about children's librarianship and strategies for broadening popular appeal. The "librarian is always in evidence; a Pandora['s] box in which may be found an answer to every question, a solution to every problem," she wrote in 1895. Newspaper announcements chronicled her frequent departures or returns from these engagements, sometimes accompanied by Bishop. Whitney would also become a well-known author of children's stories and poetry, and she wrote a song, "A Christmas Greeting to Kansas City Children," with

Reference room bustling with readers, Kansas City Public Library at Ninth and Locust Streets, 1925

composer Carl Busch, a Danish-born Kansas Citian whose work can still be found in the Library's collections.

During this period, Whitney dedicated her efforts to Library expansion, and in July 1899, the Library added its first branch. The small town of Westport had just been annexed into Kansas City, and its new Allen Library joined the Kansas City system as a standalone branch. This added more than one thousand volumes and expanded the system's geographic reach. Today, the Westport Branch—originally opened February 22, 1898—remains the oldest building in continuous use by the Library. Whitney enthusiastically welcomed the new branch, added to its collections, and immediately set out to establish a reference department, children's room, and newspaper room.

Like the Main Library, the Allen Branch hosted student concerts to raise funds for local schools as well as public town hall–style meetings about school district issues. Frequent art displays and similar events made the site a popular community gathering space. Whitney used it to expand other community connections, and the branch would soon become home to the Kansas City Historical Society. Later renamed the Missouri Valley Historical Society, the organization regularly hosted receptions at the Library. Amid that abundant community and cultural engagement, perhaps

Allen Branch, now the Westport Branch, 118 Westport Road

the most suitable praise ever uttered for the Allen Branch came in July 1913 from a four-year-old boy who passed by and commented to his caregiver, "Look, Miss Mary, that building's the dictionary."

As evidence of Whitney's stature within the profession, she was elected president of the Missouri Library Association during its annual meeting in Kansas City in October 1901. That same year, her name appeared alongside James Greenwood's in the list of editors of the six-volume *Missouri History Encyclopedia*—the first of its scope. The monthly bulletin appears to have transformed into the more substantial *Public Library Quarterly*. One issue about civic improvement was praised by the National Municipal League of Philadelphia and drew hundreds of requests for copies nationwide.

Throughout this period of growth and expansion, Whitney maintained lofty standards in hiring librarians and made wider individual contributions to the city's posterity. A *Star* article in 1897 described a fifty-question exam that Whitney expected all applicants to pass. Among other things, it requested a brief "sketch of the principal minister of Louis XIII" and asked, "What is the Bayeax [Bayeux] tapestry?" Candidates also had to translate several phrases from French into English. Five days after the original *Star* article was published, a short notice appeared: "None of the applicants for library positions passed."

Given Whitney's insistence that librarians be familiar with the classics, it is not surprising that the Kansas City Public Library also would be home to two major museums. The first was officially known as the Western Gallery of Art, but locals called it the "Nelson Gallery" for its benefactor, William Rockhill Nelson. As owner of *The Kansas City Star* and a real estate mogul, he used his fortune to tour Europe and purchase reproductions of famous works of art. The acquisition of reproductions instead of originals was a common practice at the time, intended to maximize the size and impact of new museums that had modest budgets.

Nelson's fledgling art museum completed his trifecta of ideas for uplifting the culture of Kansas City. The first was his newspaper. Second was his investment in the city's noted parks and boulevards movement. Third and most significant was a museum worthy of a world-class city. In 1897, this vision came to fruition as fifty thousand people visited the public library to see his collection of paintings, sculptures, and photographs. The collection grew rapidly in the following years, doubling the number of reproductions and adding hundreds of new pieces. *Public Library Quarterly*

Western Gallery of Art, commonly known as the "Nelson Gallery" for benefactor William Rockhill Nelson, Kansas City Public Library at Ninth and Locust Streets, 1897

proclaimed the gallery's "importance for purposes of serious and systematic study as well as for casual inspection and incidental enjoyment."

In the late 1920s, funds from the Nelson family were combined with resources from another local philanthropist, Mary McAfee Atkins, to build a museum complex, and in 1933 the Library's original collection of art was transferred to the new facility. But it is important to note that for nearly four decades, the most important gallery in the city, perhaps in the extended region, was housed in the Kansas City Public Library.

The Kansas City Museum also traces its origins to the Whitney era. When the Library at Ninth and Locust opened in 1897, the ground floor housed a museum featuring the Dyer Indian Collection. The assortment of some twelve thousand items was on loan from Daniel Dyer, a federal agent for the US Indian Agency who had worked in the Indian Territory, present-day Oklahoma, in the early 1880s. Dyer purchased or acquired items by trade from members of the Cheyenne, Arapaho, Wichita, Kiowa, Sioux, Kickapoo, Crow, Creek, Cherokee, and other Native American tribes. Included were beaded amulets, blankets, dolls, pouches, baskets, war implements, clothing, and much rarer objects, such as a Cheyenne dress adorned with 1,500 elk teeth believed to have been harvested from over 750 animals. Other objects were

Western Gallery of Art, Kansas City Public Library, ca. 1900

thought to be associated with famous individuals, including Geronimo and Sitting Bull, or with infamous events such as Custer's Last Stand and the Wounded Knee Massacre of 1890. An appraisal in 1904, the same year that Dyer converted the loan to a permanent gift to the Library, valued the full collection at $150,000 (more than $5 million today).

In Dyer's lifetime, his collection represented a cultural touchstone for Kansas City and the broader American West. Parts of it were exhibited at the World's Fairs in Chicago in 1893 and St. Louis in 1904, during a time when characters like Buffalo Bill Cody and Annie Oakley were national celebrities. The Library's museum tapped into this wider mystique and added elements of natural history and sciences, such as popular fossil and taxidermy collections. Space had to be reallocated in 1910 to expand the museum to fifteen thousand square feet (creeping into areas formerly occupied by the bindery). A full-time professional curator was hired during yet another expansion the following decade.

In 1940, the museum's forty thousand artifacts transferred from the Library's ownership to the Kansas City Museum of History and Science, which opened in the

Daniel B. Dyer Museum, Kansas City Public Library at Ninth and Locust Streets

Robert A. Long mansion the following year. More recently, Indigenous peoples with ancestral ties to the collection have emphasized that many of the objects are not mere curios or research artifacts but are spiritual pieces of living cultures. They have questioned how Dyer acquired the items and past curatorial decisions. The Dyer collection is still preserved by the Kansas City Museum, but culturally sensitive objects from it have not been publicly exhibited in many years.

Few visitors at the time would have found it unusual that Kansas City's public library housed artifacts as significant as those in the Nelson and Dyer collections. Whitney and her team transformed the Library into a leading center of cultural engagement, defining her career as well as an enduring institutional mission. In 1908, she published a history of her adopted hometown, *Kansas City, Missouri: Its History and Its People.* The book was massive: eighteen hundred pages spread across three volumes, with the first providing a one-hundred-year chronicle of the area's history and the others profiling hundreds of Kansas City leaders. On many topics, this publication remains an indispensable resource today. Whitney made room for a humble entry for herself among the biographies, where she allowed that her name had become "familiar in every household." She characteristically omitted personal details and gave readers just one real insight into her sense of identity: "Mrs. Whitney's biography is the history of the Kansas City Public Library."

WHITNEY'S PERSISTENCE, OUSTER, AND LEGACY

Just two years later, in 1910, Whitney was forced from her position at the Library. Her most recent annual report had been optimistic: "The library has become a 'civic center,' in itself, a grouping of all classes of people in search of all kinds of information." The collection neared one hundred thousand volumes. Yet a faction in the school board, led by businessman Frank A. Faxon, sought to oust her as head librarian. Faxon expressed a desire to hire "a man with modern ideas," a statement that matched the official stance of the board.

In July 1910, following Whitney's twenty-nine years of service, the board asked her to resign. "I think, since my ability to administer the affairs of the library has been questioned, that an investigation should be made," she responded. "The only treatment I ask is justice and fairness," she told *The Star.* Whitney refused to resign, and supporters circulated petitions on her behalf. Five days later, *The Star* referred to her as the "librarian in escrow." Despite the broad show of support for Whitney, some people complained about the cold atmosphere of the Library, both literally and figuratively. One patron questioned open windows during the winter, while others cited the strict rules and, predictably, Whitney's outspoken views against popular fiction. Her close relationship and cohabitation with Frances Bishop never really emerged as a public controversy, although it appears to have been a subtext in complaints that cropped up about alleged factionalism or favoritism in the work environment.

If, in her attempts to be taken seriously as a professional, Whitney was seen as opinionated, she was in good company with other female leaders judged harshly for their success. In any case, her work with children, occasional displays of whimsy, and identity as "mother" of the Library smoothed out the rougher edges of her reputation for many of her supporters. Whitney condemned the demure libraries of old, "where one must don felt slippers at the door, converse in whispers at the desk: one never talked in those libraries—where a smile was a misdemeanor."

Still, the school board maintained that a younger man with new ideas should run the Library. Whitney was offered a demotion to assistant librarian, still receiving her full salary. "The library has gotten to be a very large proposition," board president J. V. C. Karnes advised her. "It has grown away from you, and in my opinion needs for its head a person at least under 40 years of age, a scholar of eminence and distinction, who has library training and experience, and I think a man should be selected." He continued, "I have no criticism of your management, but we all have our limitations. You have done your best, and have done well, but the time has come (for the library) to take a step forward, and you make a mistake in not recognizing this." Karnes urged her to accept the demotion and spare herself the "worry and annoyances" of management as she grew older. (Whitney was fifty-six at the time.) On August 6, 1910, *The Star* reported that she had accepted the reassignment. Frances Bishop likewise was demoted to second assistant librarian.

Even before Whitney agreed to step down, Frank Faxon vowed to move carefully in selecting a new head librarian. But the choice appears to have been inevitable. Purd Wright, founder of the St. Joseph Library, had long been building his own national reputation. He was on the executive board of the American Library Association and, in 1910, was appointed to direct the Los Angeles Public Library. Faxon sent Wright a telegram on January 13, 1911, mixing flattery with a plea:

The Missourian must return, here is where he belongs, our minds are fixed, a great and fertile field is here for you, it is full of promise, no other man can do so well, we must have you, our hearts our hopes are all with thee, our hearts our hopes our prayers our tears, our faith triumphant oer our fears, are all with thee, are all with thee.

The fifty-one-year-old Wright accepted the offer to return home as Kansas City's head librarian. His formal schooling had ended after fifth grade, but he was self-educated and a prolific reader. He arrived in May 1911, decorated his office, and seemed ready to expand the legacy of the Library. Very quickly, however, he informed the board that he would not report any more progress "under existing circumstances," and in July 1912 he submitted his resignation.

Wright politely cited ill health as the reason for leaving, but it did not take a detective to uncover his real motivation. The demoted Carrie Westlake Whitney was still on staff as his assistant librarian and apparently a thorn in his side. She earned far less than her successor ($183 a month to Wright's $416). *The Star* reported that the staff had divided into factions and that "some of the employees haven't spoken to one another for months." Others, it said, communicated with one another via "office boys" who served as messengers. Wright's friends told reporters: "In his present condition the situation is beyond him unless he is given all power." He retreated to nearby Excelsior Springs, Missouri, to seek recovery in the healing mineral waters for which the city was famous.

Debate and internal investigations swirled for weeks until September 1912, when the board permanently removed Whitney. With her gone, Wright was invited back and served as head librarian until 1936. At this time, *Star* owner William Rockhill Nelson expressed his admiration for Whitney's long service in an editorial but avoided either criticism of the board for ousting her or any petition to save her job:

It is not often that a long continued term of management or a public trust leaves behind it the permanent value that has accrued to the Kansas City Public Library by reason of the thirty years of devoted and admirable service of Mrs. Carrie Westlake Whitney. . . . The funds available for the maintenance and development of the library . . . were so limited that they would have been wretchedly inadequate without the wise, farsighted and persistently cautious application of every

dollar that was allowed her. The double responsibility of providing a library for
current daily use—to meet the constant and diverse needs of the community for
edification and wholesome diversion, and to make that work the definite, solid,
worthy foundation of a collection which should endure and gain in merit with
the development of increased and constantly more discriminating requirements,
was a task of great importance to Kansas City. That was the duty assumed by
Mrs. Whitney in those far-away days and the collection of books now owned by
this community is convincing evidence of the wisdom of the board of education's
original choice of a librarian: Sensitive, alert, quick-witted, unprejudiced, except
for the best, appreciative of qualified advice, farsighted and thoroughly in love
with her work, the young librarian of thirty years ago began a monumental
service for her townsfolk.

The school board continued to pay Whitney through November 1912. Frances Bishop, no longer second assistant librarian, was demoted to working at one of the substations. Whitney and Bishop settled into an apartment at 4741 Holmes Street, in a location that is now part of the campus of the Ewing and Muriel Kauffman Foundation. For the first time since Whitney's arrival in Kansas City, she lived miles away from the Main Library. In April 1934, Whitney passed away from pneumonia at St. Luke's Hospital and was buried in Forest Hill Cemetery. She was around eighty years old.

Besides praising Whitney's librarianship, an obituary in *The Star* bittersweetly memorialized her "inseparable" relationship with Frances Bishop: "For more than 40 years these two, bound by a rare and beautiful friendship, found happiness in each other and the books of current literature with which they surrounded themselves. They dropped out of the great current, but they never lost interest in its movement and ever-changing character." Bishop died nearly nine years later in 1943 and was buried near Whitney in Forest Hill Cemetery.

After Whitney's departure from the Library in 1912, Wright reassumed leadership of an institution that had become a cultural force in Kansas City and beyond. Despite the scarcity of funds, facilities, and staffing upon her arrival in 1881, Whitney had spent the ensuing thirty-one years delivering an expansionist vision for Library services to the community. Her efforts culminated in the facility on Locust Street with two full-fledged museums, more than two dozen substations across the school system, and the branch at Westport. More important, the Library gained the trust, respect, and admiration of the people of Kansas City. This strong foundation allowed the branch system to proliferate during the early years of Wright's tenure as library director.

James Greenwood, the school superintendent, referred to the Library's growth as "manifest destiny," a concept that encapsulated the views of its founding generation. Like Whitney, Greenwood devoted his life to education and the library project; he died at his desk, "his post of duty," in August 1914. Both viewed the Library as a centerpiece of Kansas City's emergence as one of America's elite cities. In many ways, their vision was achieved as the Library transformed into a center of culture and civic engagement in a single generation.

As Kansas City grew from its frontier roots, a blank slate had allowed opportunities for innovation.

Women like Whitney and Bishop carved out professional spaces and, from scratch, pioneered aspects of library culture that proved enduring. During the Whitney era, the Library became an independent social institution and embraced the intellectual trends of the period. In no small part because of Whitney, the Kansas City Public Library emerged in the first quarter of its existence as a consequential space for the community, just as its founders intended.

When Thomas H. Swope, real estate mogul and namesake of Swope Park, died in October 1909, the thousands of mourners required an open civic space to pay their respects. His body lay in state in the community's one truly public building: the Main Library. Hundreds of local citizens filed past his casket even as other library patrons continued about their business, a perfect snapshot of the multiple roles the Library now filled. Here is where chess players, students, businessmen, women's clubs, and countless others could assemble, find information, view exhibitions, and listen to lectures. Here, they could meet the many needs of the day.

2

SUPPORTING FREEDOM AT HOME AND ABROAD

When he wants to read a book, no matter what it is about
or who wrote or published it, a citizen in a democracy goes to
his favorite . . . library and borrows it.
—ST. LOUIS POST-DISPATCH

The Kansas City Public Library's first order of business during the early years of Purd Wright's leadership was growth, and the system achieved that over his long tenure as head librarian, even as it weathered two world wars, the Great Depression, and other upheavals. Locally, the municipality it served grew rapidly as Kansas City spread outward in all directions. This expansion led the Library to embrace a series of choices that would define its values and reshape its services for a generation. By the end of the twentieth century, its approach to patron interests had transformed from the curation of materials based on community standards to advocating for the rights of each patron to follow their individual passions.

One of the most profound changes—opening library branches in neighborhood schools—promised financial thrift and better service coverage for the wider public. That strategy limited flexibility as to where the Library could expand, however, and the decision to tie branches to schools meant that the schools' structural inequalities also affected patrons' access to Library resources and services. Still, the arrangement allowed the Kansas City Public Library system to expand from one branch to more than ten during the Wright era. Economy of scale allowed it to link to national projects, supporting civic education and patriotic programs during the world wars.

Kansas City grew from a regional center to a sprawling metropolis in the opening decades of the twentieth century. Its populace—including the growing number of

Purd B. Wright, head librarian, exiting the northeast entrance of the Kansas City Public Library at Ninth and Locust Streets

Library patrons—gravitated to the commercial business districts near the riverfront, and Library services were concentrated near those and other industry and population centers. As the city's boundaries expanded, the population dispersed well beyond the Library's existing service area.

With the growth came a movement to beautify the city. As an up-and-coming metropolis, Kansas City competed directly with other municipalities for businesses, immigration, and investment. Advocates for its new parks and boulevards system drew inspiration from similar movements in New York and across the southern border in Mexico City. Notable landscape architect George Kessler provided vision while local business leaders, like metal magnate August R. Meyer, meatpacker Simeon B. Armour, and architect Adriance Van Brunt, lent political cachet. These newly landscaped areas connected the first rings of suburbs to the city. Patrons of means had the freedom to choose a living arrangement removed from the commerce, industry, and sprawling stockyards that dotted the city center and West Bottoms.

In the year after the Switzer Branch opened in a junior high school on the west side in 1911, the district's board of trustees began drawing up plans to house more branches in schools to better serve the expanding population. Wright expected questions, but the economy of the plan, he believed, outweighed any downside. The Library's first experiment with school-based branches came at Northeast and Central High Schools. Each library had space on the first floor, a separate entrance, and dedicated utilities. Additional branches soon opened in elementary schools. Wright wrote in his annual report that the decision was economic: "It will thus be possible to extend library services to a larger number of people than could be hoped for under the appropriation if an attempt were made to erect separate [library] buildings." Wright estimated that shared locations would allow for "six or seven library buildings within buildings" for the same price as "two or three separate buildings."

Wright believed that libraries within schools fit a trend of school buildings growing into multipurpose community centers, bridging divides across generations and offsetting the inherent compromises required to build a library space within a school. "It is recognized," Wright said to the board, "that it will be at first more difficult to secure use by adults of libraries located in school buildings." Over time, he assumed that schools would become places for all manner of other community services, including social work, neighborhood club activities, lecture courses, and entertainment. Wright was so confident in this prediction that he "had no hesitation in asking the location of the library branches [to be] in school buildings whenever possible . . . [to] the eastern and southern portions of the city now without book service."

As it turned out, his vision for future multipurpose community centers would unfold not in public schools but in public libraries. Without neglecting books, literacy, and education, libraries diversified to support their communities' evolving needs, and Kansas City emerged as a national leader in reaching as many readers as possible across its district.

THE FIRST WORLD WAR

Well before America entered World War I in 1917, the fighting in Europe reverberated in Kansas City. Patrons anxiously followed developments at the downtown Library. According to *The Star*, a noontime crowd of "war fans" gathered each day around a large map of Europe. Armed with newspapers recounting the latest from the front, they consulted the map to trace army movements and debate strategic maneuvers. By July 1916, this group was growing daily.

Unidentified Library visitors at newspaper racks in the reading room, 1915

When a once-reluctant United States declared war on Germany in early April 1917, the Kansas City Public Library stood ready to educate its citizens on the conflict. It had more than four hundred titles on warfare available for patrons. From that collection, Purd Wright published a curated list of one hundred "good books on the war." They "related to the war in an intimate style" and included titles from a variety of viewpoints. Notable works included first-person accounts from soldiers and nurses and literary works like John Masefield's *Gallipoli*, a poignant account of human bravery and the carnage of modern warfare. Other perspectives came from women, the American Jewish Committee, and newspaper reports. The Library furthered that public understanding by engaging Kansas Citians in community discussions about the war, its impact, and its legacy—all in the downtown Library reading room.

On August 31, 1917, the American Library Association's Library War Council designated the Kansas City Public Library as one of twelve collection centers to lead a nationwide donation campaign. The ALA set ambitious goals: raise more than a million dollars and collect hundreds of thousands of books for military libraries at training centers and on bases, naval vessels, and international outposts. Books from Missouri, North and South Dakota, Kansas, and eastern Nebraska flowed into Kansas City. The Library created a massive processing workspace in the basement of the Louis George Branch at Twenty-Fifth and Holmes Streets. Showing their patriotic spirit, librarians volunteered their time to process the donations in preparation for circulation.

National library leadership appointed Wright to direct the Kansas City Public Library's donation district, and as recruits from across the state traveled to Oklahoma's Camp Doniphan and Fort Sill and training centers in other states, books rode the rails with them. Upon arrival, reading material was organized by camp librarians from local colleges and libraries. Calls went out for periodicals and works of fiction, including books on war, popular travel, history, and biography. Among the local citizens reading the donated materials was Harry S. Truman, then a thirty-three-year-old soldier who had enlisted in the National Guard. Assigned to the US Army's 129th Field Artillery, he trained for eight months in Oklahoma, where he accessed reading materials thanks to his friends at the Kansas City Public Library.

In this effort, library leaders put out calls for "idle volumes" about recent events and books that "men will read and enjoy." Librarians urged patrons to "look through your bookcases; pick out the best you have." Service members needed books and

Louis George Branch, interior view with unidentified boy and male and female staff members, 1920

magazines "for study, recreation, and diversion in these lonely moments." Most popular were books on the war, travelogues, histories, biographies, detective stories, stories of the sea, and adventure tales. Soldiers were "men of varying tastes," and the program sought a spectrum of titles to appeal to as many of them as possible.

Camp libraries were an area of emphasis because maintaining morale was essential to the war effort. Program leaders touted books as "a stimulus and recreation for soldiers" and noted that "every nation now at war has recognized the necessity of camp libraries." Left unsaid was the often-tedious nature of warfare during this conflict, where moments of intense combat sporadically interrupted months of boring—if cautious, stressful, and uncomfortable—life in the trenches.

The Library encouraged Kansas Citians to support the war effort beyond book donations. Its War Service Money Drive generated more than $4,000 in donations in just one week in late September 1917. The Library also served as a sales location for the first round of Liberty Bonds, accounting for more than $30,000 in subscriptions. After selling Liberty Bonds directly, it promoted all additional bond campaigns. Other charitable efforts included sales of memberships in the Red Cross and of so-called

French orphan cards: holiday cards sent in lieu of traditional gifts. Proceeds supported the fatherless children of France. Posters at the Main Library and branches reminded patrons that American freedom would be threatened if the war was not won in Europe.

The global war temporarily reshaped the public's reading appetites. The demand for technical books, how-to titles, and guides on building businesses grew exponentially, while loans of fiction decreased just as dramatically. The Library's stock of books on "general efficiency" and other occupational texts frequently ran low.

Top: Interior view of the library at Camp Funston with unidentified soldiers, ca. World War I
Bottom: Exterior view of the library at Camp Funston

Unidentified staff at the Camp Funston library, 1918

Even its youngest patrons were affected. One child—formerly a regular reader—was asked why he did not come in to peruse the collection as often. He responded, "I only go to the library now when I am tired of knitting [clothes] for soldiers."

As World War I came to a halt after the armistice on November 11, 1918, the American Library Association had to figure out what to do with the 2.5 million books donated in support of service members. Coverage in *The Star* showed the scope of the problem: 32 freestanding libraries, 35 large camp libraries, and 237 hospitals and Red Cross facilities had been supplied with books. Beyond that were 651 smaller camp libraries, including 55 at aviation fields, schools, and repair depots. The navy alone had

World War I poster showing the Statue of Liberty in ruins, artist Joseph Pennell, 1918

280 stations with book collections, the Marine Corps had 65, and there were more than 1,200 smaller collections on naval vessels. The sudden surplus was offered first to the armed forces; anything that remained went to other federal entities like prisons, Coast Guard stations, and merchant marine vessels. Books donated at the downtown Library in Kansas City may have ended up as close as a cell at the federal penitentiary in Leavenworth, Kansas, or as far away as a researcher's table in Paris, France.

One of the principal aims of American propaganda during the war effort was to popularize the notion of protecting freedom by defeating the Central powers. Germany, especially, drew criticism for its aggression and authoritarianism. By supporting the war effort through books and the free exchange of information, the Library demonstrated its patriotism and commitment to freedom. In doing so, it sidestepped controversies over the government's wartime propaganda and censorship. Government posters depicted the Statue of Liberty in flames, with obvious symbolism, yet the faraway location of the conflict spared the United States from the threat of direct invasion or loss of national sovereignty. In this climate and its aftermath, what freedom meant to Americans—and to Library patrons and their reading preferences—was not always obvious.

THE PULSE OF THE CITY DURING THE GREAT DEPRESSION

During the Great Depression, the Library became a haven for community members in search of respite from the ravaged economy and a dreary world. *The Star* noted that the Main Library's reading room became "a refuge for wanderers." By 1933, the city's once-thriving Northeast community was a shadow of its former self. Millionaire's Row, an exclusive enclave of high-end properties, had mostly faded even before the worst of the Depression set in. Wealthy residents moved to Ward Parkway and the bucolic estates south of the Plaza. Left behind were pushcart vendors, flophouses, pawnshops, and, according to some, "street after street of bums." The periodical room at the Library, in the words of *The Kansas City Times*, felt "the pulse of a large city's throbbing—its unemployment and despair."

The Library's role of supporting the most unfortunate members of society, which would foreshadow its contributions to a twenty-first-century Kansas City, melded with its information service duties. Patrons experiencing homelessness rubbed shoulders with schoolchildren on field trips and businesspeople reading the latest news on the markets. Regulars gathered outside early in the morning, waiting for the janitor to open the doors. From there, the so-called "bums" would separate from the rest of the patrons, free to occupy Library spaces as long as they did not break one cardinal rule: No sleeping.

The placid scene at the Library could be deceptive for those unaware of the harsh realities of life during the Depression, but the restless, down-and-out crowds of Kansas City were not the unruly mobs that necessitated police intervention in bigger cities like Chicago and New York. And their reading habits confounded expectations: "The shabbiest will ask for the *Atlantic Monthly* . . . [the] *Nation, Forum, Fortune*, and such magazines," reported one Library staffer. Men were often caught clipping from women's magazines like *Harper's Bazaar*. Notably, down-on-their-luck patrons were free to read items of their choice and avail themselves of the same resources offered to the wealthiest and best-connected people in Kansas City, a hallmark of public library services.

In times of crisis, the Kansas City Public Library provided a lifeline for city residents as they navigated intensive economic dislocation. In return, thankful patrons brought all manner of gifts to the Library's staff: a sack of onions, a basket of flowers, a packet of seeds. This gratitude sometimes came as a complete surprise. One patron, an old bachelor, claimed that he knew his way around the kitchen. Librarians expressed doubts, which were answered the next day when the man brought freshly baked gingerbread. Despite their suspicions, staffers ate the confection and reported that it was "excellent."

LIBRARIES AND THE FREEDOM TO OFFEND

The rules of librarianship grew still more complicated with other international incidents. In May 1933, the newly formed Nazi Party launched a public campaign to burn "undesirable" books, ridding German society of what it claimed to be immoral influences. In response, *The Kansas City Star* republished an editorial by the *St. Louis Post-Dispatch* that compared the actions of citizens in a democracy with those living in Germany.

The *Post-Dispatch*'s editorial board wrote, "When he wants to read a book, no matter what it is about or who wrote or published it, a citizen in a democracy goes to his favorite . . . library and borrows it." No such opportunity existed for those in a repressive state. The freedom to read without intervention from the government was "such a commonplace of daily life that it is difficult to realize it is a privilege of citizenship in a free country."

Aside from this endorsement of free expression, there is much to learn about the changing values of Kansas City and the Library by examining the battle to determine which books were fit for the shelves. The most prominent example from the interwar years featured a novel that captured the American zeitgeist: John Steinbeck's *The Grapes of Wrath*. Steinbeck wrote his fictionalized account of the plight of migrant farmers during the Great Depression after reporting extensively on migrant labor struggles for *The San Francisco News* in 1936. The novel's harsh depictions of living standards, labor conflicts, and violence reflected the real struggles of the age.

The gritty nature of the work brought to light the tension between a library serving the community and the city's board of education. *The Grapes of Wrath*, published April 14, 1939, became an immediate bestseller. The Library quickly acquired thirteen copies, but just four months after publication, all were pulled from the shelves following a school board vote to remove the novel from circulation. The work was a sensation, its literary merits confirmed with a Pulitzer Prize, and its strengths later cited by the Nobel Prize Committee in awarding Steinbeck the 1962 Nobel Prize in Literature. Still, the Kansas City school board banned the book.

Like the debate over appropriate library content in today's America, the 1939 decision to challenge *The Grapes of Wrath* had little to do with the book's literary merits and much more to do with the board's discomfort with student access to the work's graphic nature. Kansas City's board of education was an elected body, as it had been since the school system was established in 1867. But in unique Kansas City fashion, elections were not contested on a partisan basis. By agreement, the local Republican and Democratic parties nominated candidates for an even number of spots on the six-person board. Nominations for six-year terms were approved without debate by the other party and listed without competition on the ballot. The board was thus popularly elected, but the parties controlled the nomination process, and no other candidates contested the positions.

Unlike many such bodies, the Kansas City school board had a long tradition of both male and female service, which reflected society's acknowledgment of the important role of women in child-rearing and maintaining family propriety. Social mores started at home but extended into the classroom, and both local political parties recognized women's voices as authoritative on the matter of family values. This led female members of the board to object to scenes from *The Grapes of Wrath* that depicted women during the Dust Bowl as incapable of providing for their families—within its pages, a child is stillborn, a starving father is breastfed, and those who are impoverished are forced into indecency. The scenes of struggle were significant to the narrative and reflected a harsh reality, but they posed problems for a board charged with making decisions for both the Library and the school system.

Objections to *The Grapes of Wrath* were made most vociferously by Ira Gardner, a lawyer and Republican appointee to the board. "As a father of two children, and as a taxpayer, I am especially interested in this matter," he told *The Star*. "Such an obscene, indecent book has no place in the library, and I am going to insist that it be taken out." Removal from circulation meant placing all copies in indefinite storage.

Gardner's proposed ban was the most extreme step the board could take. The head librarian at the time, Louis M. Nourse, suggested that *The Grapes of Wrath* instead be placed on the restricted list, a designation that would prevent children's access and keep the book off browsing shelves—adult patrons would have to specifically request the book. Nourse courted religious authority in his defense of the book's merits, consulting a local minister and soliciting his opinion of Steinbeck's tale. According to Nourse, the clergyman believed there were valuable lessons to be learned from *The Grapes of Wrath*. Gardner rejected this claim outright. "I would like to take that book out and read it to the minister's congregation," he said. "I'll bet he would be run out of the town the next day." The book was immoral and an affront to the community in Gardner's eyes, and he considered it his responsibility to end public support for obscene works: "If the public wants to read such stuff, let it buy it."

The community's reaction to the ban varied widely, from support to indifference, principled objection, and indignation. *The Kansas City Times*'s editorial page noted that the board's action was out of step with the rest of the nation. "Library patrons in Kansas City," it wrote, "are denied a book that circulates freely and with respect in virtually every other part of the United States." The Library itself had a tepid response. "It's a little early, I know," Nourse said, "but I haven't had much reaction from the public either way yet." Local scholars from the University of Kansas City noted a long tradition of complaints about immorality targeting such literary titans as William Shakespeare, Charles Dickens, William Thackeray, Thomas Hardy, and Henrik Ibsen. "Only time will tell how great a book artistically Steinbeck has written," said university president Clarence Decker, "but certainly his moving portrayal of certain aspects of American life should shame us into making ours a more livable country."

Others thought the ban was justified because *The Grapes of Wrath* exploited the plight of the rural poor for the benefit of the urban elite. In a letter to a local editor, Mrs. George L. Rose argued that Steinbeck's book was "pornographic from start to finish." It was, she added, "a foul slander on a brave and healthy minded people." Migrants would not like the book, she insisted; instead, its primary appeal was to "peeping Toms" in cities where people "constantly feed their eyes and hearts on coarseness."

Class divide animated an objection to the book's banishment by members of The Grapes of Wrath Committee in Kansas City. Its chair, Gordon Melvin Monroe, argued that banning the title from the public library restricted access among the poor, who could not afford it. The impact of the ban harked back to the days of Carrie Westlake Whitney, when library collections were curated for the public with the explicit goal of providing cultural uplift in a onetime cowtown evolving into a more refined community.

The dispute over *The Grapes of Wrath* highlighted a debate about the Library's purpose. Advocates for banning the work argued that community resources should not be spent on obscene content. Opposition to the ban countered that while the book's imagery was occasionally shocking, its purpose was measured edification, not voyeuristic titillation. To this group, realism was a means of fully illustrating harsh conditions, providing insight and impetus for alleviating the causes of inequity. "Instead of being condemned," wrote a Steinbeck supporter, "the book should be compulsory reading for all adults who are smug or bored or who have average or better incomes."

The battle lines in this cultural drama are familiar to supporters of modern libraries. But just as significant was the position of Kansas City's Library within the larger community. Beyond the debate about the merits and derelictions of *The Grapes of Wrath*, the board's actions had called into question its confidence in the professionalism of the staff charged with managing the Library. "The Board of Education naturally feels responsibility for the general conduct of the library," said the editorial staff of *The Star*, "but it cannot act as a committee to pass on every book bought." Instead, "it is the board's function to employ a competent librarian and to allow him to manage the library in accordance with general rules and policies." The act of banning such an important work impugned the standing of librarians and brought "unfavorable notoriety" to the city. Ultimately, if the Library was only permitted to circulate books suitable for school district students, *The Star* concluded, "Kansas City has no public library."

In May 1940, the Library—and Steinbeck—prevailed. Ten months after the work was banned in Kansas City libraries, *The Grapes of Wrath* won the Pulitzer Prize. The following month, a board member, Dr. Hester Wilson, moved to reinstate the book into circulation and place it on the Library's restricted list, off the shelves and off-limits to children. Ira Gardner wanted it to remain banned and threatened to read excerpts from the work publicly at the next board meeting. "These people say it is fit for the public to read," he said. "I'm going to read some of the smutty passages of that book and let them decide whether or not it should be in our public library."

The next school board meeting became contentious as Gardner railed against Steinbeck's work. *The Star* reported that he shouted, "*The Grapes of Wrath* are rotten fruit!" Gardner proceeded to read at length from the work, emphasizing passages he believed were vulgar, obscene, and anti-Christian. "The book is tainted with filth, indecent stories and foul words of the brothel house," he said. "The scum on the jar has gone from cover to cover of the book. As spoiled grapes are discarded because they are rotten, so should foul books be kept from the library shelves when they are spoiled by the indecency of their contents."

Other members of the board reacted with unease at the spectacle. Members sat with flushed faces, hands on their heads, nervously drumming their fingers on the table. At one point, Butler Disman, who opposed the ban, asked, "Is there anything worse than that in the book?" to which Gardner replied, "Yes, do you want me to read some more?" Before Disman could answer, fellow board members protested that they had heard enough. The only one persuaded by Gardner's antics, Annette Moore, maintained that since the Library was funded by the school levy, it should only provide materials appropriate for the city's youth. When the vote was cast, the final tally was 4–2 against the ban. *The Grapes of Wrath* returned to circulation, albeit on the restricted list.

Annette Moore, upper right, with other members of the Kansas City school board, five years before *The Grapes of Wrath* controversy, 1934

The Star called the compromise a "sensible solution." The book would not be available to children or visible to uninterested adults. The fraught process, *Star* editors hoped, would caution future boards to avoid "unwarranted interference in the rights of readers." The Library emerged with its reputation at least somewhat restored, and all thirteen available copies of *The Grapes of Wrath* were quickly checked out, with reservations taken for a holds queue.

This single episode is significant, revealing not just the long history of debate in this city about literary content, especially in an age of heightened political pressure, but also the tensions within the Library about control. Arguments about banning books would continue in Kansas City, if not with the level of vitriol experienced in neighboring communities. But the real issue was the independence of the public library and how the city valued it. It simmered as the Library became a proxy in determining shared civic values.

Before that conversation reached its climax, however, a second global confrontation—with the authoritarian Axis powers of World War II—sparked a renewed wave of library patriotism.

BOOKS ARE FOR VICTORY

When Japan invaded Manchuria in 1931, most of Kansas City was too preoccupied with the Great Depression to pay heed to the events in South Asia. By the time that Adolf Hitler's Third Reich annexed Austria, muscled the West into accepting the annexation of the Sudetenland, and sparked open warfare in Poland, all of America understood the danger. Once more, a war in Europe had drawn its attention. And once more, despite rising instability across the globe, debates raged about the strategic and moral implications of America entering the fray. As in the First World War, the Kansas City Public Library answered the call to duty, first in supporting the Allied war efforts and later by sending materials and people to the theater of conflict. The fight over books and censorship at home turned out to be a precursor to the battle for freedoms abroad.

On December 7, 1941—two days after the Library celebrated its sixty-eighth birthday—aircraft from the 1st Air Fleet of the Japanese Imperial Army Air Force launched a devastating surprise attack on US naval forces at Pearl Harbor. What President Franklin D. Roosevelt famously termed "a day that will live in infamy" drastically changed the world. In Kansas City, residents woke up to shocking Monday morning headlines. *The Kansas City Times* blared, "JAPANESE BOMBERS RAID U.S. ISLANDS." Evening readers learned from *The Star* that Congress had voted to declare war on the Empire of Japan. In response, Japan's allies, Germany and Italy, declared war on the United States. America answered in turn.

As it did during the First World War, Kansas City's library stood ready to support US troops with reading materials wherever they were stationed. Louis Nourse and other librarians across Missouri met in Jefferson City two weeks after the attack on Pearl Harbor. Supported by the Red Cross and the United Service Organization, they began a drive for troop reading material—the Victory Book Campaign. In Kansas City, individual donors brought books to the Library from home libraries across the city. One resident, Helen Minaker, was captured in a *Star* photo spread making her contribution to a smiling Patricia O'Brien, an assistant library clerk. The wall behind O'Brien was covered in posters from the Library's most recent call for donations, one depicting a soldier reading in the trenches and declaring, "Yanks in Germany want more Books." In addition to libraries, donation bins were placed at schools where citizens were required to sign up for ration cards. Eventually, there would be donation drop-offs for books throughout the city, especially on dedicated Victory Book Campaign donation days.

The business community backed its patriotism with advertising dollars and used valuable print space to promote the book drive. Harzfeld's Department Store ran advertisements and hosted a "Victory Book Depot." Chasnoff Furriers asked, "Won't you help 'arm' our men with books?" These firms made sure that people in Kansas City encountered the drive even if they seldom went to libraries, placing book drops in prominent locations throughout the metropolitan area. One advertisement from John Taylor Dry Goods did double duty. First, it encouraged Kansas Citians to donate. "The boys in the service want books," it proclaimed, "surely every household has some it can contribute." Second, the ad conveyed the types of books that soldiers, sailors, and marines most wanted through a clever illustration. Small caricatures—one from each branch of the service—stood reading books from the most popular genres: westerns, mysteries, and adventure books. Safeway Foods got into the spirit of the drive with the likeness of a uniformed soldier reading beneath a tree next to that week's prices for Libby's tomato juice.

Coverage of the drive filled pages of *The Kansas City Times* and demonstrated the community's commitment to the project. Landon Laird wrote in his regular "About Town" column that he witnessed an eight-year-old who "marched up to the service desk of the (Library's) Central branch and deposited a picture book, *Airplanes of the World.* 'This book was my best Christmas present and I'm crazy about it,' he volunteered, 'but I believe some of our soldiers fighting . . . might like to see it, too.'"

Elsewhere, a woman in a limousine had her chauffeur drop off close to one hundred books. "My name's not important," she said, refusing any credit for her donation. Rabbi Samuel S. Mayerberg dropped off a large bundle of books with a handwritten note stating simply, "God bless you."

Laird found a few lighter moments amid the earnest campaign. One "donation" turned out to be a long-overdue (and mildewed) library book that had sat forgotten for ten years in a basement. Another librarian reported an unusual reference question. A woman appeared at the Main Library's front desk and asked for "all the information you have on the Navy." Flabbergasted by the scope of the request, the librarian asked for more details. The patron replied, "I'm going to marry a Navy man and I think I should know what I'm getting into."

Civic organizations did their duty, too. The Optimist Club met for its regular luncheon at the downtown Hotel Muehlebach on Friday, January 30, 1942. In addition to indulging their appetites and sharing a positive outlook, members decided that each would donate a book to the campaign. Two hundred books were collected, with a pledge for three hundred more coming from J. P. Willis, the club's chair. The Mantle Club, a fraternal organization, donated an estimated ten thousand books delivered in "motor cars and light trucks" to the basement of the Louis George Branch for sorting and shipping. Due to this massive community effort, the Library was inundated with books and invested a lot of staff time in sorting, stamping, and packing the materials.

Though the initial Victory Book Campaign ended April 1, 1942, the larger effort to donate books to the war cause continued. President Roosevelt's declaration of a Victory Book Day revitalized a flagging donation effort, and by the end of the year, the national drive had delivered more than ten million volumes. The pace of donations picked up the following year. First Lady Eleanor Roosevelt announced the start of the 1943 Victory Book Campaign in a syndicated column, using her "My Day" editorial as a printed corollary to her husband's famous fireside radio broadcasts. "This is the day on which the Victory Book campaign starts," she wrote. "There is one thing which every one of us can do, no matter how busy. We can go through our bookshelves and send . . . the books which we feel will be enjoyed by the officers and men in the army, navy, marines, and merchant marines." The First Lady wrote from firsthand experience: "I found in Great Britain the boys in hospitals wanted every possible kind of book. . . . All of them need entertainment, and the detective or western story, full of thrill and excitement, will take them out of the moment."

Others were trying to use library books to make sense of a world of which they knew little. "Books of travel, historical novels, and all books that are up to date, will be interesting to the men in our armed services," Roosevelt wrote. She asked people to think about the service members and do what they could to help. "If you were far away from home," she said, "books would be the things that would mean the most to you in your leisure time. So, think about those who defend us in camps, on ships and on fighting fronts all over the world, and let's get busy and provide the biggest collection of victory books we have ever had in this country."

Kansas City heard the call. On the Saturday following her announcement, local leaders from the Library, the United Service Organization, and the Red Cross met at the Hotel Muehlebach to discuss the 1943 edition of the Victory Book Campaign. Chairman O. A. Greer suggested a goal—two hundred thousand volumes—but stressed that the nature of the reading material was more important than the number. During the 1942 campaign, "many citizens . . . denuded their attics and basements of volumes long ago discarded," he said. "The result was quantity without quality." For 1943, the committee asked citizens to add "a personal touch by signing names on the fly leaves and possibly penning messages that will remind uniformed men who read the books that home folk who do not know them personally have their welfare at heart."

Greer, Kansas City mayor John B. Gage, and committee member Fred Goldman discussed the campaign across the airwaves on WDAF radio's evening broadcast.

American War Dads Convention, with O. A. Greer seated at front right, September 17, 1946

The roundtable chat again emphasized the inclusion of personalized messages in donated books and stressed the importance of relevant reading. As Greer told *The Star*, "Virtually any volume that has appealed to its owner sufficiently to make him desire to keep it will be acceptable." *The Kansas City Times* reported, tongue in cheek, that "the slogan of the nationwide campaign this year is 'Praise the Lord and Pass the New Edition.'"

The Kansas City business community aligned its message with the campaign's. Woolf Brothers clothiers ran an advertisement pointing out the link between books and the freedoms that Americans cherished. Giving books, the ad claimed, was "one way to give thanks that you're not forced to read *Mein Kampf*," Adolf Hitler's infamous autobiographical manifesto. The Kansas City retailer Emery, Bird, Thayer and Company likewise encouraged Kansas Citians to do "your part for the Victory Book drive! Share your best reading with the Men in the service and keep up their morale!"

Kansas City's youth also provided crucial reading material for America's fighting forces. "Pupils pile up books for men in service," read a *Star* headline. Elementary students donated more than five thousand books in 1943. Teachers created visual aids to help the youngsters track their contributions. At the Fairmount School, classrooms had charts showing an airplane race; the more books donated, the farther their plane advanced in a race against their peers. Students at the Humboldt School held paper and candy sales, raising funds to purchase sixty "pocket-sized" books. More than sixty-two thousand students in Junior Red Cross chapters in elementary and high schools coordinated the youth collection campaign.

The Associated Press reported on April 26, 1943, that over 4.5 million volumes had been donated to the Victory Book Campaign. Despite this effort, requests from service members and their organizations reflected additional demand, and the drive continued. Even the planned two years of donations were not enough to meet the need. On June 2, 1943, the board of the campaign extended the drive for "as long as the requests last." According to Paul Bader, a representative for the drive, the armed forces were still requesting 250,000 books a month.

The impact of the Victory Book Campaign often reverberated back to Kansas City. David M. Nelson, a sergeant stationed at Camp Sibert in Alabama, reached out to a local couple, the Immeles. He found their address on the mailing label of a donated magazine and offered a quick note of gratitude. "Today I walked into the supply room and picked up a magazine [and] found some pictures and notes that

I had been particularly interested in," he wrote. "I just wanted to thank you for my being able to read that issue. I had been overseas and over there I was not able to read many newspapers or magazines." Mrs. Immele forwarded the note to *The Star* with the hope that it "might make others want to give more" to those in the service.

Closer to home, Victory Books were an integral part of soldiers' well-being at Fort Riley, Kansas. "Books will help us win this war," wrote the novelist Kenneth S. Davis, who was reporting for *The Star*. "They maintain morale and broaden the mental horizons of the individual soldier, [and] books are real ammunition in our fight against the regimented anti-culture of the Axis hordes." Davis drew this conclusion after visiting soldiers, librarians, and staff at the fort. "Contrary to a quite popular conception," he said, "the cultural life of the individual does not end with his entrance into the armed forces." The army—through Victory Books and other programs—provided not just entertainment but also a sense of shared meaning.

The need for books, to the novelist Davis, was evidence of a diversity of thought that boded well for America's fate in the war:

The chief function of the rigid army "system," with its uniforms, its drilling in groups, its clear definition of levels of authority, is of course to submerge individuality, to subordinate the individual to the group so that the unit of action becomes not the individual man, but the platoon or the company or the regiment. No doubt this is essential to success in battle. But there seems to be in the army today a sincere effort to avoid the complete sacrifice of individuality. There seems to be a belief that though the soldier's physical life must be pretty much regimented his mental life, for the good of our democracy, should not be.

Books became frequent metaphors for democratic values in Kansas City. W. M. Reddig, *The Star*'s book editor, gave a speech titled "The Battle of the Books" at an American Legion post. Its members had gathered to celebrate collecting over one thousand volumes. "The Victory Books are well named," Reddig told the crowd. "They are fighting books. They are messages from home to the boys in the camps, on the ships, on the fighting fronts. They are powerful, ideological weapons from the arsenal of democracy, the greatest arsenal of its kind in the world."

Reddig contrasted Victory Books with the indoctrinating tactics of the German Third Reich. "The Nazis are supposed to be the masters of ideological warfare," he said. "It is true that they have a very effective technique, but they don't have the ideas and they don't have the writers to compete with the democratic camp." His speech highlighted the difference between substance and form. The fascists had a compelling facade but no foundation. American ideas, in contrast, were messy and sometimes coarse, but the strength of the system was its diversity and capacity to manage disagreements without resorting to the German practice of book burning.

Public book burning by the Nazis was communicated to newsreel viewers throughout the world and decried in a somber display at the Kansas City Public Library. *The Star* took note as well. "Freedom of press and the printed word is one of the four freedoms guaranteed the United Nations by the Atlantic Charter," it wrote. "This was one of the first inalienable rights that Hitler violated when, on May 10, 1933, he caused 25,000 volumes to be consigned to an enormous bonfire" in front of the University of Berlin. Other instances of book burning took place across Germany, including events where children were told, "As you watch the fire burn these un-German books, let it also burn into your hearts the love of the Fatherland."

The Victory Book campaigns organized by the Kansas City Public Library contrasted America's drive to enrich and expand awareness with the Nazi urge to purify the minds of the people through the destruction of the printed word. At the Main Library, a display highlighted books by Jewish authors and other prominent writers, from Karl Marx and Sigmund Freud to Jack London, Helen Keller, Upton Sinclair, and Ernest Hemingway. The Library displayed these and other burned volumes side by side with works proclaimed as "weapons against Hitlerism," many addressing the world war and others considered to be "outstanding contributions to the cause of public enlightenment." Among them were Richard Wright's seminal works *Native Son* and *12 Million Black Voices*. The Library celebrated the fact that while our enemies in war destroyed books, Kansas City cherished those same texts as testaments to the freedom of expression. They were emblematic of the values of intellectual freedom and ideological plurality that defined American democracy.

The Library's efforts to expand liberty during wartime had a local focus. *The Star* pointed out how the institution "aid[ed] in Home Defense" by circulating "Pamphlets Tell[ing] Housewives How to Help." The Library also created a special information desk that covered various topics related to gardening, rationing, nutrition, and conservation. It offered "accurate information for every citizen," drawing clear connections between individual consumer actions at home and the larger socioeconomic forces shaping the world at war. That was reinforced by *The Star*, which wrote, "The housewife should know when she buys more than her immediate needs require of sugar or canned goods that she is paving the way for a future rise in prices and a consequent inflation." Minimizing domestic needs not only prevented inflation from crippling the war efforts but also defended the American way of life.

While the war could seem far away, the Library emphasized the role that proper home economics played in preparing local households for hardships. Victory Gardens were a common way for families to avoid rationed goods and still ensure nutritious meals, and the Library curated multiple pamphlets on gardening for the novice. More sobering were warnings about the ravages of war on the home front. "The major casualties of any national crisis or war," *The Star* warned, "are never to be found in the list of soldiers and sailors wounded or dead, but in a sickly, starving population." The Library answered that concern, the newspaper said, by lending "books on good food for people with low incomes." Those guides to "making do" with limited resources became universally applicable when war rationing affected the city.

The Library also felt the impact of the war in more direct ways. Many of its alumni served in the fight. John Rankin Greenlee, the Library's chief of stacks, maintained an honor roll, devoting a page to each military volunteer in a ledger customized with an American flag and silver star stickers. In those pages, Greenlee also pasted newspaper articles about the soldiers, sailors, and marines who had answered the call to active duty. More than 170 names were listed, along with scrapbook coverage of the conflict and the Library's role in the war.

The Library not only tracked the military careers of its former staffers, but it also sent them congratulatory correspondence. Each listing in Greenlee's honor roll included an updated mailing address, and he and other Library staffers penned Christmas letters. Margaret Cline, Library switchboard operator, illuminated the missives with watercolor paint, and they included greetings from Harold Hamill, who took over as head of the Library in 1943. The letters prompted appreciative replies.

The honor roll included Jeanne Gallucci, a former assistant at the Library who had trained in Washington, DC, and served as an American Red Cross worker in Norman, Oklahoma. Also among those listed were Dorothy Cutting, who served as a librarian at Fort Riley, Kansas, and Pvt. Susan Harris of the Women's Army Air Corps in Coffeyville, Kansas. They and many other women served with distinction and were acknowledged, along with their male counterparts, for putting their careers and lives on the line for their nation.

The honor roll also tracked losses. Seven former employees were killed during their service in global conflict:

- Glenn J. Frazier worked as a page during high school, enlisted in the navy, and became an ordnanceman, second class. He went missing in the Pacific theater in March 1945.
- Pvt. Leonard J. Giaramita, who served in the Army Corps of Engineers, died January 6, 1945, in Belgium. He had worked as a page in the reference department in 1942.
- Lt. William R. Lennox, a Library page from 1935 to 1937, served as a navigator in the Army Air Corps. He died in an accident during advanced radio and gunnery training in Tucson, Arizona, on February 6, 1943.
- Lt. Glessner Reimer had worked in the Main Library stack room. A P-47 Thunderbolt fighter pilot, he arrived in England in April 1943 and went on to earn the Air Medal with four oak leaf clusters and a Purple Heart, participating in more than sixty air missions. He died in action over Vire, France, on July 30, 1944.
- Lt. Warren Staley served as a page in the Library's reference room from December 1939 until he resigned to join the army in December 1940. He perished along with other members of his B-25 flight crew in the South Aegean Sea in February 1944. Staley originally served in the army's 110th Engineer Battalion before transferring to the Air Corps.
- Ensign Frederick C. Tothill, who served as a Library page in 1938, lost his life after bailing out of an aircraft during carrier-based operations off Kyushu, Japan, on March 18, 1945. Tothill entered the navy in 1940 and earned his flight wings and commission as an officer in 1941. His heroics earned him the Distinguished Flying Cross and a Silver Star for action over Iwo Jima.
- Lt. Harold Vaughn worked as a page at the Library's Blue Valley Branch. He enlisted in the Air Corps and was training to become a fighter pilot when his P-39 crashed outside Klamath Falls, Oregon, on December 31, 1944.

PROTECTING PATRONS WITH
UNPOPULAR IDEAS

The Library's service to the armed forces during the Victory Book Campaign set a high-water mark for support of the military that would be hard to replicate. Subsequent conflicts, from Korea and Vietnam to the Gulf War, did not command the same level of national focus as World War II. The Kansas City Public Library has always been a partner to the community it serves, and when that community is divided, the Library's response has reflected those uncertainties.

At the same time, it has established itself as a place where patrons can safely explore unpopular ideas. The early banning of books, such as *The Grapes of Wrath* episode, became anathema to its best practices after World War II. Having supported the defeat of fascism, it made little sense to librarians that public institutions would limit patron access to ideas. Book bans and challenges in classroom settings occurred sporadically throughout the United States. But by the 1960s and 1970s, the bulk of bans on books came in nations like Rhodesia and South Africa, where the likes of James Baldwin and many other American authors saw their works banned for inciting racial animus. Amid the Cold War, the Soviet Union also gained notoriety for controlling so-called "dangerous" ideas through bans and other restrictions. It was against this form of information control that free speech advocates and opponents of book banning framed their protection of even radical ideas as patriotic.

As a publicly funded institution, the Library protected access to information of all stripes—a role that became critical to its modern success. In 1985, the *Star* editorial board sounded the alarm about a growing effort to challenge books. "Taste is a matter of private evaluation," it wrote. "Morality is a matter of personal conscience." In 1990, the Greater Kansas City Coalition Against Censorship hosted events throughout the metropolitan area and set up displays at the Kansas City Public Library. The Library had long supported Banned Books Week, an annual American Library Association campaign celebrating the freedom to read. It has been especially vocal in recent years as America's cultural and political divisions spilled into school and public libraries and as challenges of books and other literary materials surged.

The Library's commitment to freedom—of speech, reading, and expression—came under strain at a public event at the Plaza Branch in May 2016. Longtime Middle East envoy Dennis Ross spoke on historical US-Israeli relations, then took questions.

A local Jewish-American activist, Jeremy Rothe-Kushel, was first to the microphone, and his remarks suggested that the two countries had engaged in state-sponsored terrorism. After Ross responded, Rothe-Kushel followed up once and then attempted to speak again before being grabbed by a private security guard employed by one of the Library's partners in the event, the Jewish Community Foundation of Greater Kansas City. The guard was joined by others in a security detail composed of off-duty police as Steve Woolfolk, the Library's director of public programming, attempted to intervene on the patron's behalf.

Rothe-Kushel was arrested for trespassing and resisting arrest despite Woolfolk's insistence that the Library encourages public discourse and did not wish to have the person removed. Police then arrested Woolfolk (who suffered a torn knee ligament in the process), and he was charged with three counts, including interfering with an arrest. Library Director Crosby Kemper III decried the security team's response as "an egregious violation of First Amendment rights."

The incident, and notably the Library's defense of free speech, drew national attention. Julie Todaro, president of the sixty-thousand-member American Library Association, maintained in a statement that libraries "are public institutions that serve as catalysts for public discussions that help solve community challenges. Such efforts are not possible when patrons are not allowed to engage in open debate in a public forum, but rather are arrested for asking difficult questions."

The two charges against Rothe-Kushel eventually were dropped, but the case against Woolfolk moved ahead as the Kansas City Police Department and Jackson County prosecutors held firm in their support of the arresting officer. Sixteen months of legal wrangling ended with a bench trial in municipal court in September 2017 and a quickly delivered verdict: Woolfolk's acquittal on all counts. "I don't understand how this kind of thing could happen at a public event," Judge Joseph Locascio said in handing down his ruling. "You're going to have people say ridiculous things at a public event. . . . You scratch your head and move on."

Woolfolk's response at the outset of the episode and steadfastness through the legal aftermath earned him the 2017 Lemony Snicket Prize for Noble Librarians Faced with Adversity. It is awarded annually by the bestselling author and the American Library Association to individuals who have "faced adversity with integrity and dignity intact." The ALA also presented the Library with its Paul Howard Award for Courage for "unusual courage for the benefit of library programs or services."

An arrest and public trial are extreme examples, to be sure, but the Kansas City Public Library has always sought to serve the interests of its community. Early in its history, that meant bringing what the Library perceived as the best elements of culture to the masses. During the 1930s, efforts to ban books highlighted the tension between that charge and demands on the school system to regulate appropriate content for children. In times of war, the Library moved mountains of books to provide reading materials for service members—as both a practical and ideological commitment to American democracy.

As the twentieth century wore on, the Library understood that service to the community could best be upheld by promoting free speech and protecting an individual's right to pose difficult questions. The journey from banning books to promoting Banned Books Week might seem incongruous, but the Library showed a consistent belief in the people it served. At home and abroad, at war and in peace, and often when it was uncomfortable and unpopular, the Library continued to support, nurture, and protect its community.

3

FROM SEGREGATION
TO INCLUSION

The Kansas City Public Library is committed through its practices, programs, collections, and services to creating and fostering an environment of equity, non-discrimination, and pluralism, grounded in respect and appreciation.
All Individuals are welcome regardless of race, color, age, national origin, sex, religion, disability, sexual orientation, gender status or identity, marital status, or political affiliation.
By fostering an atmosphere of diversity and inclusion, we will continue to be leaders in public discourse, address current and future community needs, and inspire a community of readers.
—KANSAS CITY PUBLIC LIBRARY POLICY STATEMENT, 2021

The Kansas City Public Library of today is thoroughly devoted to the values of diversity and inclusion. Born of a city with southern roots, however, the Library is not fully distanced from the community's history of segregation.

In her annual Librarian's Report in June 1885, Carrie Westlake Whitney claimed that the "persons who visit a public library vary as much as the books on the shelves." This sentiment of inclusiveness endured throughout the Library's long history, but the Library's historical policies and its gaps in services to the community did reflect the biases of the times. Those community biases narrowed over the course of the twentieth century, however, as the Library strove to become more welcoming, equitable, and intent on serving all in the public.

The rapid expansion of its branch system, starting in 1911, presented a fundamental dilemma. The Library upheld nondiscrimination policies, yet nearly all of its new branches were located in racially segregated school buildings. Further, professional librarians at white schools and in the Main Library were white, and even at what were often called the "Black branches," Black librarians frequently faced obstacles to professional development.

Ursula Fiona Fuhri, the head of reference services at the Kansas City Public Library from 1976 to 1985 and a graduate of the University of Missouri's library science program, noted that the values of the Library in the early twentieth century were inextricable from those of the city: "Kansas City has always exhibited an amalgam of northern and southern attitudes; the example of the public library and the school district, both under the control of the same Board but only the latter segregated, illustrated this clearly."

GARRISON SQUARE AND LINCOLN BRANCHES

As in the real estate market, the factor that most affected library usage was the location of its buildings. When Purd Wright became head librarian in 1911, his first goal was to "extend library service to the community at large rather than to the few." His plan entailed many new branches to supplement the Main Library at Ninth and Locust Streets and what was then the lone branch at Westport. Eleven branches were established between 1911 and 1916, followed by nine more in the 1920s and '30s. Among these was the Garrison Square Branch, which opened on December 26, 1914.

Located inside a city recreational facility, the Garrison Square Branch represented the first sustained effort by the Library to serve the African American community. The building, which also held a gymnasium, clubroom, and showers, occupied a public park at Fifth Street and Troost Avenue. Checkout of books in the first six months totaled a healthy 7,721 volumes. Libraries were not frequently mentioned in local Black-owned newspapers, but in 1915, one of them, *The Kansas City Sun*, noted, "To the busy worker our free public libraries, art galleries and museums, which are now opening their doors to evening visitors, offer splendid advantage for picking up knowledge." The same publication praised Director Wright for his support of the Garrison Square Branch, calling it the best facility of its kind west of the Mississippi River.

Persuading the community to visit the branch was never easy. In 1915, branch librarian N. Etheline Wilson reported that she did not see many adults in the building due to long workdays that left residents "little time or strength for reading." As a result, she and her staff focused much of their work on children and youth outreach, which became a Garrison Square signature. In an area with low literacy rates, it remained a challenge to increase engagement with the Library and its resources, but tailoring the collection to the neighborhood paid dividends. Works by Black authors proved especially popular. As reported in *The Sun*, a private donation in 1915 also funded a subscription to *The Crisis*, the NAACP's official magazine, established five years earlier.

The branch would be affected by the city's demographic shifts; in the late 1910s, many of the neighborhood's Black residents moved south, whereas recent immigrants from central Europe and the Middle East moved in. Community use of the Garrison Square Branch continued to decline until 1922, when it relocated to Lincoln High School.

Garrison Square Branch interior with students

For all the early importance of the Garrison Square Branch, the library at Lincoln High deserves special attention. Opening in 1922 at Nineteenth Street and Tracy Avenue, it provided continuity as the only library location specifically serving African Americans anywhere in the state of Missouri. References to this branch in the Black press, especially *The Call*, the city's leading Black-owned newspaper, were highly favorable. Amid the calamity of the Great Depression, Kansas City maintained Lincoln Branch activities when few other cities offered any services to Black residents and taxpayers.

The economic bust brought pay cuts to all district employees. Teachers and librarians feuded over budget decisions, book purchases declined by one-third, and hours were reduced significantly. *Paul Jones Magazine*, a local Black-owned publication, nonetheless celebrated the Library in this difficult time and even singled out Purd Wright for praise in October 1931: "The colored people of Kansas City, Missouri, should be profoundly grateful to Mr. Wright and other good citizens. . . . There are but few cities in this country which have established libraries for the exclusive use of the colored people."

Lincoln Branch entrance at Lincoln High School, 1925

Lincoln Branch interior, 1940

Wright's progressive leanings were well known, extending to his friendship with renowned *Emporia Gazette* editor William Allen White. White ran an anti–Ku Klux Klan gubernatorial campaign in Kansas in 1924, and in a letter to Wright (after running as an independent and finishing third in the race), he thanked the librarian for his unflagging encouragement. White continued:

> *I am happy, and sustained by a joyous feeling that I made a good fight and that I have registered a decent vote as a protest against the bigotry of the Klan, which threatened the rights of four groups of our citizens, the Jew, the Catholic, the colored people and the foreign born.*

Wright's backing of the Lincoln Branch was unusual for a city like Kansas City. By 1930, it held more than fifteen thousand books. A decade later, *The Call* reported that a "visiting sailor" declared the branch's collection as being on par with the Schomburg Collection of Negro Literature and History at the New York Public Library. Although the sailor overstated his case, the Library undoubtedly modeled itself after the famous New York institution. During this period, the Lincoln location provided outreach services, partnering with nonprofit organizations, interracial committees, and church groups, and it hosted book talks and exhibitions. Lincoln staff provided regular book services to the privately operated African American Wheatley-Provident Hospital and the Niles' Home for Orphan Children.

Lincoln librarians, most notably Priscilla Burd, assisted with a Black history course at Lincoln High. Burd, who was white, came to the Kansas City Public Library in 1922 and started at the Lincoln Branch in 1926. She previously had worked for libraries in Iowa and for the YMCA and the American Library Association's Library War Service in France around the end of World War I. Along with Lincoln High teacher W. R. Howell, she started an African American special books collection (later named the Dr. John F. Ramos Jr. Collection in honor of the first Black member of the school board). There is little question that the Lincoln Branch held one of the more substantial Black book collections in the region—comparable to that of Lincoln University in Jefferson City, Missouri, the first of the nation's historically Black colleges and universities (HBCUs) to grant a degree.

STAFFING THE "BLACK BRANCHES"

In a "Work with Negroes Round Table" discussion hosted by the American Library Association in 1923, director Purd Wright upheld Kansas City's approach to library services, emphasizing that Lincoln was the only such facility serving Black people anywhere in the state. In the ALA report that followed, Wright said he considered separate branches the best way "to reach the Negro with books and public library service best suited to the different communities." He maintained that Black citizens in Kansas City received the same library services as white residents and, using the language of the day, however problematic, said "there was no Negro problem west of the [Mississippi] River."

Despite that insistence, a 1930 article in *Library Journal*, the primary trade outlet for the field, questioned why there were no Black head librarians at the Lincoln Branch. Wright responded: "[We] have never found an efficient colored one." He acknowledged, however, that Black librarians "have never been admitted to the [library] training class," offering that in Kansas City, "a Negro could never work at main or at a white branch."

Against those limitations on professional advancement, Black librarians still rose to prominence. Capitola Jones, daughter of the editor of *Paul Jones Magazine*, is considered to be the first professionally accredited Black librarian employed by the Kansas City Public Library. Her paternal grandparents had been enslaved, and her father was the first Black lawyer licensed in the state of Missouri. Capitola (alternatively spelled Capitolia or Capitolita) worked as a children's librarian from 1931 until she passed away in 1967. She was active in the National Association for the Advancement of Colored People, spoke to gatherings of numerous organizations, and befriended local Black celebrities, including jazz musician Cab Calloway.

Wright retired in 1937, by then in his late seventies, leaving the question of equity in hiring and staffing at the Library unsettled. Irene Gentry served two years as interim director before Louis M. Nourse was appointed to lead the system in 1939.

Top: Lincoln High School administration, including branch librarians Mildred Kimbrough (front row, far right), Priscilla Burd (second row, far right), and Capitola Jones (third row, far left), 1937
Bottom: Capitola Jones, Mildred Robinson (née Kimbrough), and Lois Payne working the front desk, Lincoln Branch, 1954

Almost immediately, the Library's hiring practices arose again as a public issue. As Nourse was working on the libraries-in-schools expansion plan and *The Grapes of Wrath* controversy, the Negro Chamber of Commerce requested that the Board of Education place a Black librarian in charge of the Lincoln Branch. When it was rebuffed, the chamber organized a protest outside Library offices in 1940. Nourse relented and appointed Mildred Kimbrough (later Robinson), a graduate of Lincoln High, the University of Toledo, and the Hampton Institute Library School, in early 1941. By this time, the high school and the public library branch had moved to a new facility at Twenty-Second Street and Woodland Avenue.

During Nourse's tenure, questions about staffing policies were accompanied by concerns about library services to minority communities. A study by the National Urban League noted that more than 70 percent of Kansas City's Black residents, twenty-nine thousand of forty-one thousand, lived in the Paseo district near Lincoln High School, but the city's African American population outside that area was not specifically served by any branch. White students, meanwhile, also had wider access to library resources in classroom or school collections.

These issues, among others, fell to Richard B. Sealock, who would spend eighteen years as Library director beginning in early 1950. Nourse had stepped down some eight years earlier and was succeeded first by Priscilla Burd, followed by Harold Hamill. Sealock had been the head librarian at the Gary Public Library in Indiana. When he finally came aboard in Kansas City, *The Kansas City Times* expressed hope that he would bring the Library back into the American Library Association's good graces.

First on his agenda was assessing the branch structure. In 1952, a study by the Kansas City–based nonprofit Community Studies Inc. indicated inefficiencies in the branch setup and pointed to a combination of good intentions and underlying racial biases as at least partly the cause. The report identified the need for a branch at the intersection of Independence and Prospect Avenues, potentially replacing the Lincoln Branch. Indeed, over fifty-one thousand people lived within a mile of the intersection and were not served by a branch. But before considering a new facility, the study's authors advised, the expansion of adult education in the neighborhood was needed. "Negroes, Italians, and Caucasian Americans, many of low socio-economic level . . . cannot be expected to make immediate and extensive use of a library," they said.

Another service gap was identified in an area near Twenty-Seventh and Prospect, with a Black population of nearly fifty-four thousand people. It was conveniently located near the north–south Prospect Avenue and east–west Twenty-Seventh Street bus lines. The report was hopeful that "segregation patterns" could be overcome with a Library branch there and, when combined with adult education programs, it would improve community literacy levels. As with the previous proposal, however, the report warned without evidence that "Kansas City Negroes have not proved to be good readers."

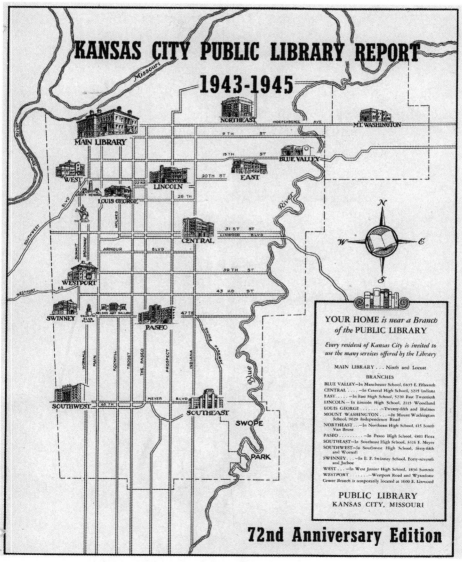

Map of locations of the Main Library and branches, 1943–1945

Beyond racial divisions, branches often saw little socioeconomic diversity. The Blue Valley Branch, for example, was in a heavily industrial area at Fifteenth Street (now Truman Road) and Winchester Avenue. Less than 3 percent of the neighborhood population of more than twelve thousand had completed a high school education, and local residents, largely African American and Polish, rarely visited the location. Usage statistics here were among the lowest in the system.

Library director Richard B. Sealock standing with unidentified woman, ca. 1950

Top: Jackson School, which housed the Blue Valley Branch
Bottom: Interior of the Blue Valley Branch

The Center Branch, located in the Jewish Community Center at Linwood Boulevard and Wayne Avenue, posed a different dilemma. Its neighborhood was residential and the most densely populated of any area surrounding a library—and it ranked highest in the Library's service district in average academic achievement. Known as the Jewish Institute Branch from 1913 to 1936, then as the Center Branch until 1961, it was, along with Lincoln, one of two locations that explicitly served minority patrons. While its demographic factors should have made it one of the most active branches in the system, Center consisted of "only one small room" and lacked signage outside the building to attract visitors. The Jewish Community Center was preparing to move south, following the Jewish population shift, and for that reason the Library was reluctant to invest further in the neighborhood.

At Thirty-Second Street and Indiana Avenue, the branch in Central High School offered a counternarrative. The school was restricted to white students even though Black families were moving into the area in increasing numbers. As the 1952 report from Community Studies described it, "the racial characteristic of this area is changing faster than patterns of segregation are being eliminated." The report stated that Black residents could not use the library branch because, although the library was officially

Jewish Community Center, 1989

Central High School Branch entrance

unsegregated, the school itself was still segregated for white students only. Most neighboring African Americans traveled to the Lincoln Branch instead.

The report recommended moving the Central High School Branch elsewhere in anticipation of continued population shifts and declining usage. History intervened. Kansas City's schools began integrating formally in 1955, a year after the Supreme Court's landmark ruling against school segregation in *Brown v. Board of Education*, resulting in the student body of Central High School shifting from all-white to almost all-Black by 1962. The library at Central High School remained open as a public branch until 1986, serving far more Black students than adults.

A final location that survived the 1960s, despite shortcomings identified in library reports, was the West Branch at Eighteenth and Summit Streets, in West Junior High School. The neighborhood was populated by a mix of Mexican American, African American, and white residents. Like the Blue Valley Branch, the West Branch struggled with low educational levels and low adult readership—challenges exacerbated by the Library not offering materials of specific interest or use to the community. Gaps in library service for this community, especially a lack of Spanish-language materials, would not be addressed until new resources allowed for a full restructuring of the branch system in the 1980s and '90s.

"HOLE IN THE DOUGHNUT"

The analyses of problems and proposals for the Library's future led to two significant developments during Sealock's time as director: the 1956 passage of bonds to construct new library buildings and an escalating series of conflicts over the Library's approach to serving racial minorities. The bond measure, approved by voters by a four-to-one margin, was to provide a new Main Library and two major branches, one on the Country Club Plaza and the other at Linwood Boulevard and Tracy Avenue. The latter was intended to replace the "Black branches" at Lincoln and Paseo High Schools. Only the Main Library and Plaza Branch were constructed.

In the wake of the Supreme Court's *Brown* decision, the population of the Kansas City school district, and consequently that of the Library's service area, shifted rapidly to include more Black families as white residents abandoned several neighborhoods within the district's boundaries. Driven by migration from southern and border states, Kansas City's Black population increased from 41,500 to more than 83,000 between 1940 and 1960. By the end of the 1960s, some 45 percent of students in the Kansas City school district were Black—a demographic transformation that extended to Paseo High School. The Library operated a location in the school, but like many similarly positioned branches, it was less accessible to adult patrons and eventually closed in 1968.

The Lincoln Branch suffered from a similar lack of investment during this period. The school library moved within the building, the public library branch shut down, and the space was filled by a student media center in the summer of 1967. These closures were expected with the plan to open a new voter-endorsed branch. But more than a decade had passed since the 1956 bond issue. No construction of a replacement branch took place, leaving a massive gap in service.

Meanwhile, plans for the new Main Library downtown moved swiftly to fruition. The old building on Locust Street—constructed in 1897 and last expanded in 1918—had long been overcrowded, and by the 1950s, space constraints limited the development of specialty departments, maintenance costs were growing, and the lack of parking made the location less convenient by the year as automobiles continued to displace public transportation.

Opening in 1960 on Twelfth Street between McGee and Oak, the new Main Library fit the expectations of the "space age." The architecture was starkly modern, with a rectangular glass-curtain construction and an abundance of aluminum. The Library occupied seven floors, from two basement levels up through level five. The school district occupied floors six through eleven. Inside, the Twelfth Street entrance opened into an expansive lobby that featured a marble mosaic floor with library-motif panels. Most of the remaining floors offered a practical and popular mid-century solution—off-white vinyl tile. The interior layout was flexible—different departments separated by bookshelves rather than load-bearing walls—to accommodate changing needs in the future. The children's library was accessed through a separate entrance off McGee Street.

Main Library at Twelfth and McGee Streets, 1960

Next came the Plaza Branch, which opened in October 1967 at Brookside Boulevard and Main Street, the previous location of the E. C. White School. It was the largest in the system, boasting robust services, events, and circulating collections. The airy design featured walls of windows surrounded by white quartz arches and a sweeping view of the picturesque Plaza.

As welcomed as these two signature facilities were, concerned citizens became vocal about the Library's inability to build a new branch for the Black community. Less than a year after the opening of the Plaza Branch, in the summer of 1968, Kansas City again hosted the American Library Association's annual conference. Given the social context in America in this period, the gathering was expected to bring attention to racial divisions in the Library, school system, and city at large.

The scrutiny started a few weeks earlier when a *Library Journal* article aired allegations by a recently resigned Library staff member, Carol Turner, and a request from the Library's staff association that the school board should investigate. Turner, who had completed her training at Rutgers University two years earlier, sent a letter to the board. As reported in *The Star*, she accused Sealock of controlling decision-making on each book order, purchasing "old books," and acquiring books that he thought the public "should read rather than what it wants."

Additional allegations suggested that Library services lacked inclusiveness due to the service gaps in impoverished neighborhoods, that it did not carry enough popular foreign-language periodicals, and that there were not enough adult education programs for the illiterate. Several of these factors had been cited in the Library's own studies as reasons not to establish branches in particular neighborhoods. Turner also accused the Library of lacking an organizational chart, resulting in every small decision being made by the senior administration. Inequalities in staff compensation and excessive staff turnover rounded out the list of complaints.

Sealock curtly responded, "It is not even worth commenting on." That did not dissuade *Library Journal* from continuing its examination, and just days before the ALA conference, it published an article titled "The Hole in the Doughnut" by Thorpe Menn, the book review editor of *The Star*. Accompanying it was a second article, "The School Board that Played Public Library" by Gordon Stevenson, a former librarian and administrator.

In Menn's description of the "hole" in Library services, he noted that two branches "in the inner-city ghetto, are not open to adult patrons. Poor people, presumably, don't read!" He blamed the longstanding policies of the school board, which he said "remained a tight little island of reaction to growth, clinging to its possession of its library as something preciously its own." Accentuating those inner-city deficiencies, Menn said, was a near circle of effective library services provided by the Kansas City, Kansas Public Library and the Johnson County Public Library to the west and south and the Mid-Continent Public Library to the north, east, and south on the Missouri side.

Stevenson's piece covered many of the same themes, but he more directly alleged racism by the school board and Richard Sealock. He claimed that the Library's services

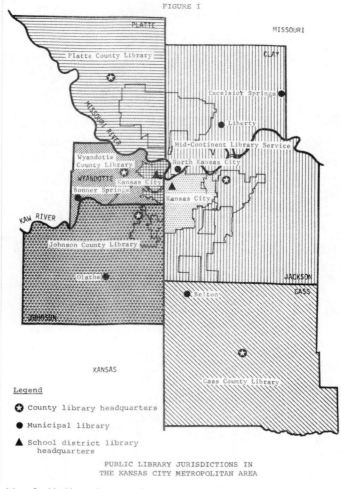

FIGURE I

Legend

⊗ County library headquarters

● Municipal library

▲ School district library
   headquarters

PUBLIC LIBRARY JURISDICTIONS IN
THE KANSAS CITY METROPOLITAN AREA

Map of public library districts in the Kansas City metropolitan area, February 1966

to schools were "20 years behind the times" and those to the public even worse. Most seriously, he directed attention to Superintendent James A. Hazlett's recent request to transfer control of $450,000 from the Library to the schools—money that for twelve years had been earmarked for the still-unbuilt branch at Linwood and Tracy. "Service to the Negro community is in serious jeopardy," Stevenson said, and "in a heavily populated, deteriorating neighborhood that needs help desperately."

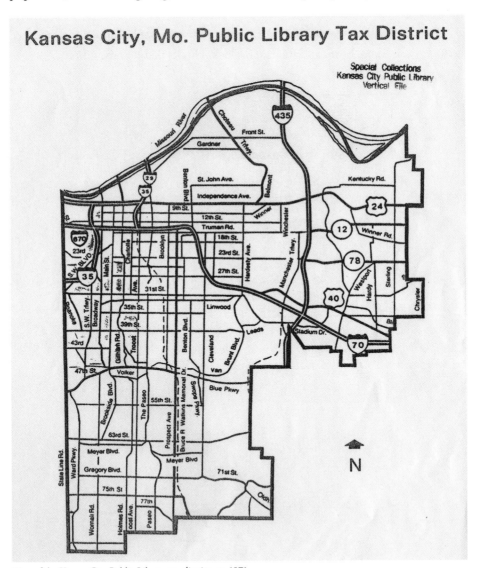

Map of the Kansas City Public Library tax district, ca. 1971

Library leadership tried to justify the construction delays. In September 1967, for example, Sealock told the school board that a branch in the Linwood-Tracy area "would be subject to problems not conducive to use of [the] library or to staffing it." Saturdays, he continued, "would be a problem day. We are largely staffing our libraries with young women." In February 1968, *The Star* reiterated Sealock's hesitance, which it attributed to the "change in the neighborhood's clientele. The area has shifted primarily from white to Negro in recent years."

The director of the Mid-Continent Public Library, James A. Leathers, told *The Times* that if the location were in his

Dr. John F. Ramos Jr., the first African American trustee of the Kansas City school board

district, he could establish a branch in ninety days. He also believed federal funds would be available if Kansas City were to seek them from the state librarian. Indeed, State Librarian Charles O'Halloran confirmed that money was available and said the Library could get an initial grant of $100,000 to increase neighborhood services.

Stevenson concluded his article with a critique of the makeup of the school board, which was not representative of its constituents. Five of the six members lived in one neighborhood, and only one, John Ramos, was a person of color. In 1969, a new system for selecting school board members was implemented to improve representation of the entire district. A year later, three Black members joined the board. Stevenson hoped that the newly constituted panel would finally separate the Library from the school system: "Metropolitan library services are more than a luxury, they are a vital part of the business, social, economic, and cultural fabric of the city—or they should be."

The Library undertook internal discussions about the responsibilities of local engagement and the impact of national events. Like other cities across the country, in the spring and summer of 1968, Kansas City was torn by the assassination of Martin Luther King Jr. The tragedy ignited protests in which six Black residents died in clashes with police. The mayor convened a Commission on Civil Disorder, and its final report noted that the racial integration of local schools had stalled. The commission recommended expansion of the school district throughout Jackson County to reincorporate the white families who had left. This measure faced political complications and ultimately floundered amid a decades-long lawsuit.

As pressure intensified, the Library responded with reforms to its outreach efforts. In July 1968, *The Kansas City Times* reported on plans to cosponsor traveling story-telling and film programs for children and teens. The Library also opened a room, staffed by college students, in the Wayne Miner subsidized housing development, with two thousand residents. The Library worked to complete a new room in the Boys' Club at Forty-Third Street and Cleveland Avenue, and in October of that year, a small branch opened at Forty-Eighth and Prospect. *The Times* continued its reporting on the issue, claiming that these developments, however welcome, were due more to the efforts of the state librarian's office, which had pushed hard to extend "library services to the oft-times bookless inner city."

The changes to the Library's portfolio in the summer and fall of 1968 were of an impermanent nature and not enough to help Richard Sealock keep his job. He resigned under pressure in October amid a planned investigation by the school board, and he was replaced by Stephen Kirk, the Library's head of history collections and acquisitions and, most recently, its supervisor of branches.

INCLUSIVE LIBRARIANSHIP

Sealock's departure, during one of the most tumultuous years in postwar America, paved the way for a fundamental shift in library services as a spirit of inclusion was infused into the mission of the Kansas City Public Library.

In December 1968, Kirk initiated talks with the Mid-Continent Public Library system about reciprocal lending agreements to broaden the reach of services to the Kansas City Public Library's diverse patrons. Kirk also accepted the $100,000 grant offered by the state library (later renewed for a second year) to improve outreach services. The Library connected with the Inner City Health Agency on Truman Road and proposed opening summer Library stations at the St. Mark's Church at 1101 Euclid Avenue and the Holy Name School at 2210 Kansas Avenue to promote educational materials on African American culture. The Library had already purchased $12,000 worth of books for the project, and Kirk sought additional input from community members who had expressed concerns about the lack of services in the area. Free films were shown at forty city parks and recreation sites six nights a week, and the Library partnered with the Model Cities Program and other social services agencies to open a service outpost in the Linwood Multipurpose Center in 1970.

The Kansas City Star noted that Kirk permitted ideas from the staff, long "bottled up," to come to fruition. Initiatives ranged from film screenings, story hours, community forums, and youth programs to the development of materials on Black history, preschool programs, and outreach to the elderly. The forty-three-year-old director also had the kind of magnetic personality that smoothed over a tense relationship with the school board—and proved no less effective in his personal life. Kirk would meet his wife Charlotte Wornall, a library assistant and descendant of the prominent John Wornall family, while working at the Kansas City Public Library. Once, in a debate over yoga, they retreated to the stacks behind the social science desk and Kirk demonstrated that he could stand on his head for fifteen minutes. Aside from charming his future partner, his enthusiasm for the "contemplative experience" of yoga remained a visible part of his public persona.

In February 1970, the school board purchased land at Twenty-Third Street and Chestnut Avenue for a temporary Lincoln High School–area branch—in a neighborhood that had gone three years without public library service. The plan called for the construction of a prefabricated building with nine thousand books and several study spaces to serve the community's immediate needs. School board member John Ramos supported the location, and with assistance from the Model Cities Program, the building opened as the Benton Branch in 1971, remaining in operation until 1988.

At the same time, Kirk received funding from the school board for a workshop to train staff to work with illiterate patrons, placing a special emphasis on service to members of the African American community. The Library celebrated Negro History Month in February 1971, and several special exhibitions included works from Black artists and books from the African American–centric Ramos Collection. The Library also made microfilm available from Black newspapers published across the Midwest. In total, these activities were enough to gain important recognition for the Library in the Negro History Bulletin.

This effort to expand representation and service coverage for racial minorities was notable considering the long history of unequal access within the school district and city. Kirk, for instance, would run into strong headwinds when the Library requested an increase in the tax levy in 1972. A *Kansas City Times* editorial articulated the history of grievances and the limited nature of the new programs. The future of those initiatives was not guaranteed, but the author argued that "Kansas City will be under strong moral obligation to follow through." In fact, it said, "it is difficult to understand why the library did not initiate these services years ago." The paper criticized the Library for failing to build a full-service branch in the Lincoln or Linwood neighborhoods. "During the long years of neglect," it concluded, "readers in the inner city . . . have largely had to fend for themselves. More often than not, this meant that they did not avail themselves of any library services at all."

Adding to this public frustration, tight budgets caused the school board to seek funding increases for schools and the public library. Kirk enthusiastically backed the proposal, admitting that both the schools and libraries had unresolved issues of racial discrimination but maintaining hope that voters would see enough progress with recent changes to support a higher tax levy.

The conversation was more difficult than he anticipated. The Kansas City chapter of the Southern Christian Leadership Conference (SCLC) and its executive director, Emanuel Cleaver II, soon weighed in. Cleaver wrote a letter to Kirk in June 1972, expressing "concern over the lack of adequate library facilities in the black community" and wanting to know "the plans and goals of the library system as they specifically relate to the black community." Cleaver reminded Kirk that the 1956 bond issue, passed sixteen years earlier, resulted in construction of the Plaza Branch but not the promised full-service branch in the inner city.

Kirk responded by detailing the Library's expanded efforts and explaining that the higher levy would increase the budget by about $240,000, an amount sufficient to maintain buildings and services, increase staff salaries, and expand the book budget, but not enough to construct new facilities. Concluding on a note of conciliation, he explained that Black patrons were increasingly utilizing the Plaza and Main libraries. Cleaver's reply, two days later, returned to the unbuilt branch, stating, "I must interpret this fact to mean that once again the black community has been ignored and taken for granted." Regarding the smaller library stations and new services, he added, "I view those simply as gestures of tokenism, in order that a semblance of concern and progress might seem to be achieved, while in actuality we are being denied a total library for which bond money has been approved."

Their correspondence received coverage in local media, and the Kansas City chapter of the SCLC openly campaigned against the increased levy on the August ballot. The proposed levy measure narrowly failed, opposed by a little more than 52 percent of those who voted. Undeterred, the school board voted to place the same proposal on the upcoming general election ballot. This time, Kirk opposed the measure, reasoning that the Library first needed to rebuild its image and gain the trust of the community. He insisted that all future proposals for increased taxes clarify how the funds would be spent to benefit the entire community.

Kirk's warnings about the second ballot measure, and its ultimate failure with voters, demonstrate that he understood the concerns about how the Library served the people of Kansas City. Practically, however, the rejection of the levy left him without enough money to maintain existing services, much less expand into underserved parts of the city. Recognizing impasses on tax revenues, system consolidation, and independence from the school district, Kirk submitted his resignation on December 5, 1972. He reiterated his previous statements favoring separation of the Library from the school district and explained that he was leaving because it "is very difficult to slow down and talk of cutting book budgets and reducing staff." Kirk left the library field entirely and pursued other business opportunities with import manufacturers in Kansas City.

The board named Idris Smith, an employee of forty-five years, acting head librarian in January 1973. She had worked at the West Branch, then in the Main Library's reference department, and finally as supervisor of the Main Library. After a national search, Harold R. Jenkins, director of the Lancaster Public Library in Pennsylvania, was named head librarian in late 1973. Despite what seemed like endless fiscal uncertainty, the Library continued to make changes to better embrace Kansas City's cultural diversity. It opened the Seven Oaks Branch at 4416 East Thirty-Ninth Street, in a shopping center of the same name, in 1974. Jenkins procured a grant from the Missouri State Library to create a neighborhood information center, and much of the programming related to community health and education.

In 1975 and 1976, the Library partnered with the newly established Black Archives of Mid-America to conduct fifty-six interviews for an oral history project centering on the African American community. The recorded conversations, still available today through the Library's Missouri Valley Special Collections, preserved the stories of prominent Black citizens, including civil rights activist Alvin Brooks, former Kansas City mayor and current US Representative Emanuel Cleaver II, trailblazing city council member Joanne Collins, and barbecue master Ollie Gates. In two years as director, Jenkins had come to understand "there is a lot of black history in Kansas City that has not been . . . written about and no one is ever going to do it . . . if immediate steps are not taken to correct this situation."

The Library's Black studies librarian, Rose S. Bell, provided administrative support for the oral history project and sought advice from the Schomburg Center, Harvard University, and the Inman E. Page Library at Lincoln University in Jefferson City, Missouri. The Kansas City Association of Trusts and Foundations lent support through a grant. Bell, Jenkins, and Black Archives founder Horace Peterson expressed a desire to continue the project "indefinitely," expanding it to hundreds of interviews. As Jenkins noted, one of the key benefits of the program was "an improved image (of the Library) in the eyes of all citizens of the black community."

SAFE SPACE IN THE SHELVES

Under Jenkins's directorship, the Library increasingly recognized and embraced a movement for acceptance, civil rights, and liberation that extended beyond the Black community. In 1967, reference librarian Donna McBride took an interest in a patron who, according to newspapers, "was known at the Kansas City Public Library as, 'that woman' who collects those books." She was Barbara Grier, a noted activist associated with the lesbian rights organization Daughters of Bilitis and a writer for the first nationally distributed lesbian magazine, *The Ladder*. Grier was no stranger to libraries, having worked at the Kansas City, Kansas Public Library when she first moved to the area, and her then partner Helen Bennett worked for the University of Missouri-Kansas City libraries. Grier's own bibliography, *The Lesbian in Literature*, was part of the Kansas City Public Library's collection, and McBride frequently used it as a reading guide. The two eventually started a relationship and became lifelong partners.

If the experience of McBride is representative, tolerance toward diversity in sexual orientation at the Library was more prevalent by then than in many other urban systems. As one example, McBride recounted an incident in which a shelving employee had verbally harassed her for being a lesbian. Jenkins, as director, supported McBride, and the offending employee was let go over the incident. McBride later recalled that at many, if not most, workplaces in the 1970s, the threats and potential loss of her own job "probably would have scared me to death, and he (the tormenter) would have gotten away with it." Supporters understood, in the words of one activist in 1964, that "perhaps it's a bit too early to invite public libraries to carry a lesbian magazine," but the Kansas City Public Library bucked the trend and carried this material.

In 1973, Grier and McBride started a publishing company, Naiad Press. It released one book in its first year while the couple continued their day jobs. By 1983, they had moved to the warmer climate of Tallahassee, Florida, and published the press's first popular book, *Curious Wine* by Katherine V. Forrest, selling four hundred thousand copies. That was followed two years later by their most controversial—and, not coincidentally, most successful—book, *Lesbian Nuns: Breaking Silence*. Its two coauthors, who were former nuns, conducted fifty interviews for source material. Catholic officials protested an interview with the writers that would appear on local Boston television, leading to the episode's cancellation. This censorship gave the book an even more tempting (if unofficial) tagline: "Banned in Boston."

Grier's and McBride's experiences at the Kansas City Public Library in the 1970s helped shape their publishing careers. Naiad Press went on to publish five hundred books, all initially more popular in private bookstores than in libraries. After retiring in 2003, the couple sold their company to Bella Books, and they wed once same-sex marriage became legal in California in 2008. When Grier passed away in 2011, McBride fondly remembered, "Her goal in publishing was to make lesbians happy about themselves."

PROGRESS AMID STRUGGLES

For all the value of these initiatives, emerging technologies increasingly supplanted civil rights and equity as the chief budgetary concern for libraries nationwide. During the civil rights movement of the 1950s and '60s, the Kansas City Public Library had missed opportunities to restructure and diversify, and now, when it was ready to embrace inclusion as a guiding value, the economic and political circumstances of the day slashed its budget. After surpassing 250 full- and part-time employees in

1971, the payroll declined by more than one hundred people by 1982. The anti-tax sentiment affecting the school district and Library extended into the 1980s as Kansas City voters rejected a 1986 bond issue that would have established four full-service branches and finally ended the awkward public-libraries-in-schools arrangement. Nonetheless, during these years of pronounced fiscal challenges, the Library continued to make headway in the effort to better connect with underserved communities.

For example, it was in this period that the Library expanded its services to Kansas City's long-neglected Latino community. Through much of the first half of the twentieth century, people of Mexican descent made up most of the Latino population in Kansas City. Around 1950, people from Central and South America and the Caribbean region began to arrive in Missouri. Drawn to the railroads and stock-yards, they settled on Kansas City's West Side or in the Armourdale and Argentine neighborhoods on the Kansas side of the state line. In education, Hispanic students were often segregated into the Adams School at Twenty-Third and Mercier Streets or funneled into vocational institutions (or the workforce) before secondary school. Between 1911 and 1926, the Switzer Branch, located in a junior high school, served the West Side population. In 1927, the West Branch replaced it, and it remained in operation until 1988.

Irene H. Ruiz, left, standing with branch manager Julie Robinson, tenth anniversary celebration of the Ruiz Branch, September 30, 2011

Starting in 1976, librarian Irene Ruiz almost single-handedly transformed library services to the Hispanic community. Born Irene Hernández in 1920, she grew up in San Antonio, Texas. During World War II, she worked for the US Office of Censorship as a translator and monitor for phone calls between the United States and Latin America. After the war, she earned her teaching certificate from Our Lady of the Lake University in San Antonio in 1948 and, following her marriage to fellow teacher Francisco H. Ruiz in 1956, pursued additional educational opportunities at Texas Tech, the University of Kansas, and Vanderbilt. The couple moved during the 1960s to Lawrence, Kansas, and then to Kansas City, where Irene taught Spanish in secondary schools. She entered the library science program at Emporia State University in 1969 and taught in the evenings as an adjunct English professor at Penn Valley Community College from 1971 to 1976. She transferred to Lincoln High School, then to Martin Luther King Junior High School, and finally joined the Kansas City Public Library in 1976.

Ruiz served as the West Branch librarian until her retirement two decades later, following the facility each time it relocated—from West Junior High School to a retail area at 902 Southwest Boulevard in 1988 and then to 525 Southwest Boulevard in 1995. In her role, she collected Spanish-language books, reference materials, and films to address the dearth of materials of interest to the West Side community. "Books open up a new world to you," she later explained. Ruiz also identified a second glaring oversight: There was no historical account of Kansas City's Hispanic communities. Between 1977 and 1982, she conducted oral history interviews, many in Spanish, of sixty people, focusing on the lives and family stories of community members from the 1920s and '30s.

Adding to Ruiz's work was a 1977 donation to the Library's Missouri Valley Special Collections of a cache of records from the founder of the West Side Guadalupe Center, Dorothy Gallagher. The board of directors of the community and social service center provided additional materials in 1983, helping the trove to span the history of the Hispanic community over much of the twentieth century. Today's Guadalupe Centers Inc. has continued to partner with the Library on public programming and other presentations. An exhibition at the Central Library, *Kansas City's Guadalupe Centers: A Century of Serving the Latino Community*, celebrated the organization's one hundredth anniversary in 2019.

When Ruiz retired in October 1996, she did so humbly and rejected any celebration or even public acknowledgment. The greatest sign of her impact on the community came as people noticed her absence, calling on her to "unretire." Marie Hernandez, a Kansas City resident, wrote to *The Star* about the "great loss for the West Side Community. . . . I take this loss very hard." She continued, "Ruiz's direct influence prompted me to continue my computer education, to improve my writing skills, to study Spanish grammar and to vote . . . it was she who directed my children to all sorts of interesting bilingual books and as a result, they both were reading four or five books a day. We need her back." In the end, Ruiz's intangible contributions touched as many members of the community as her diversification of book collections, branch operations, and oral histories.

Notwithstanding Irene Ruiz's modesty, a substantial portion of the community wanted to celebrate her contributions to the city. In 2000, the Library's board of trustees set up a citizens' committee to select names for a new West Side branch at 2017 West Pennway Street. The committee made three recommendations, and the board selected Biblioteca de las Americas (Library of the Americas). But in June and July, a grassroots campaign demanded that the Library name the location after Irene Ruiz to honor her commitment to the community's Hispanic heritage. When a petition exceeded five hundred signatures, the board agreed and altered the name to Irene H. Ruiz Biblioteca de las Americas.

The branch opened on September 10, 2001. Five days later, as the nation mourned the tragedy of 9/11, the Library celebrated the new facility. "Part of terrorism is to terrorize and disrupt, and we just didn't want to allow it to ruin all of this," Director Daniel J. Bradbury explained. The Library had finally separated from the school district in 1988; it was the first time since then that a new building had been named in honor of an individual. Irene Ruiz continued to volunteer for children's story time for more than a decade after her retirement, and she passed away September 3, 2023, at the age of 102.

The Ruiz Branch is not the only testimonial to the work of a noted contributor to Kansas City's minority communities. In 1988, the Library named its new branch at 3050 Prospect Avenue after a legendary newspaper editor and civil rights leader, Lucile Harris Bluford. "It's a strange feeling," Bluford said of the decision. "It's an honor; you wonder if you can live up to it." A columnist in *The Star* quickly corrected her: "We are of the opinion that the library will have to live up to Bluford's name and her record of accomplishments as a journalist and civil rights leader."

Bluford was born in North Carolina on July 1, 1911, and blessed with unusual educational opportunities for a Black child of that era. Her father, John Henry Bluford, was a professor at North Carolina Agricultural and Technical University. In 1921, the family moved to Kansas City, where her father taught science at Lincoln High School and Lucile attended Wendell Phillips Elementary. Later, as a student at Lincoln High, she dove into journalism by working on the school newspaper and yearbook and entered politics through the student chapter of the NAACP and the

Lucile Bluford attending the opening of the eponymous Lucile H. Bluford Branch, 1988

student council. She also made her first connections to *The Call,* one of the largest and most important African American newspapers in the nation, where she would eventually spend nearly seven decades as a reporter, editor, managing editor, and, after the passing of owner Chester Arthur Franklin in 1955, part-owner and publisher. Because of racial discrimination, she was barred from enrolling in the University of Missouri's journalism school and pursued her bachelor's degree in journalism from the University of Kansas, graduating in 1932.

Bluford spent a summer at the Black-owned *Daily World* in Atlanta, then returned to her hometown to work for the *Kansas City American,* another Black-owned newspaper, and shortly afterward, *The Call.* By 1938, she was managing editor and applied to the University of Missouri's graduate journalism program. Her application was provisionally accepted in January 1939, but when she attempted to enroll in person, the school denied her entry because of her race. With backing from the NAACP, she filed suit in 1940 and saw *Missouri ex rel. Lucile Bluford v. S. W. Canada* (named for the university registrar who blocked her entrance) reach the Missouri Supreme Court. Its judges upheld the university's denial but ruled that Lincoln University, an HBCU, had to establish a master's program by February 1941 to accommodate Bluford and other Black students. An undeterred Bluford refused to accept the facade of a "separate but equal" program at Lincoln University and continued to apply to MU without success.

At *The Call,* Bluford documented anti-segregation boycotts and sit-ins in the 1950s and '60s, during a time when white-owned newspapers seldom covered the Black community in favorable terms. Roy Roberts, managing editor of *The Star,* was quoted as saying, "We don't need stories about these people." In this climate, Bluford lobbied successfully for the Public Accommodation Ordinance of 1964, which outlawed segregation in public spaces in Kansas City.

Twenty-three years later, Bluford still worked sixty-hour weeks for *The Call* and was a widely respected advocate for racial equality. She maintained modesty about being the namesake of a new Library branch but recognized and enthusiastically supported what the facility meant to the Black community. At the groundbreaking ceremony on September 1, 1987, Bluford donned a hard hat and dug the first shovel of dirt. She remarked that Black residents were once not allowed in Kansas City's public libraries, a statement that was not accurate but nonetheless reflected the history of de facto segregation in the Kansas City Public Library's employment practices and its unofficially designated "white" and "Black" branches. A year earlier, Bluford had editorialized in *The Call* in favor of the ballot measure that provided funding for the branch.

Her long familiarity with library issues resulted in bittersweet sentiments about the branch, the Library system's first newly constructed facility in more than twenty years. Bluford expressed pride, calling it "a storehouse of knowledge" and saying "the works there can help everyone." The new branch and three others then under construction would replace nine older facilities, consolidating services and serving a broader, more diverse swath of the community. The others were North-East at 6000 Wilson Road, West-Independence at 11401 East Twenty-Third Street, and South at 201 East Seventy-Fifth Street. Upon their completion, 95 percent of the Library district's residents lived within two miles of at least one of the system's branches or the Main Library.

Lucile Bluford also understood history, noting that the new library had long been needed in the Black community. "This place was promised to this area a long time ago," she said, "and we're just now getting it." When the building opened July 30, 1988, she had waited more than thirty years since the original passage of bond funds for a full-service branch on the east side. On opening day, Bluford was the first patron to enter the branch and the first to borrow a book.

Reverend and Mayor Emanuel Cleaver II, speaking at the Kansas City Public Library, June 12, 1998

Her achievements and accolades continued to accumulate: an honorary doctorate from the University of Missouri, the institution that had shut its doors to her six decades earlier, in 1989; a distinguished service citation from the University of Kansas in 1990; and recognition by the Greater Kansas City Chamber of Commerce as Kansas Citian of the Year in 2002. Bluford passed away June 13, 2003, and in 2016 the state of Missouri declared her birthday, July 1, as Lucile Bluford Day.

The opening of the Bluford Branch in 1988 marked the Library's long journey from participation in segregation, all too common in Kansas City, to a full embrace of racial inclusiveness. It can never be said that the work of desegregation is finished or that the values of inclusivity and diversity are fully realized, but this fitful history shaped the Library in significant ways. Looking back, Congressman Emanuel Cleaver II recalls that when he first came to Kansas City in the early 1970s, "it was in the library where my consciousness was awakened." But "the thing that drove me crazy," he says, was that this "center of enlightenment . . . was not available to all people." Now, Cleaver says, "the library has become what I always wanted it to be."

4

INDEPENDENCE AND THE ENDURING COMMITMENT TO CHILDREN AND YOUTH

*Our story hours are advertisements for the books we have in
the library . . . the children are told a story and then they want to
know the name of the book and who wrote it. In that way they
get into the habit of reading . . . books that build up character
and become their life-long friends.*
—CHILDREN'S LIBRARIAN ELLE TOUGH, 1915

ligning Library services to Kansas City's communities of color was a developing effort that took time to achieve. The same could not be said of the Library's leading-edge outreach to children. As early as 1897, when the Main Library at Ninth and Locust opened to patrons, city youth received innovative reading support at every opportunity. When Library branches opened in schools in the early twentieth century, they deepened the resources and support available to students.

But by the mid-twentieth century, the connection proved challenging as Kansas City's school board struggled to meet the operational needs of both a major public library and school libraries. These tensions culminated in the Library's separation from the school district in the 1980s, a move that proved beneficial to the Library's ability to serve the entire community more equitably.

Today, service to the city's youngest patrons is a source of pride for the Kansas City Public Library. But it is important to recognize that most early public libraries did not design their spaces or services for children. Kid-friendly book lenders were rare enough that they made national news. In 1895, *The Kansas City Star* reprinted a report from *The Chicago Inter Ocean* about Herbert Putnam, the new director at the Boston Public Library. Putnam, who would go on to become the librarian of Congress, introduced several changes that became industry best practices, including a reduction in the number of books locked away in closed stacks, the installation of time-saving pneumatic tubes for processing book requests, and most significantly the creation of a juvenile department. This specialty unit allowed children to browse age-appropriate books without request slips or card requirements. In an age when many children's titles were thought to contain little literary merit, Putnam advocated for more of them. Promoting such open access and highlighting the value of illustrated children's books was novel, but in a *Kansas City Times* article in 1895, Putnam insisted that "pictures are a means of instruction," and he continually promoted an environment that favored access over restraint.

In Kansas City in 1897, Library Director Carrie Westlake Whitney oversaw construction of a new building—the first in the city dedicated primarily to library use—incorporating several of Putnam's ideas. While opening closed stacks to browsing would have to wait, her outreach to young readers made the Kansas City Public Library a leading-edge institution. For example, parents, teachers, and librarians had long known that summer vacation posed a challenge for young students. Learning gains often "melted" during the long, warm days. Summer learning programs were an antidote, known to keep students engaged and bridge the learning gap between the end of the spring term and the start of fall, improving educational outcomes. As early as 1904, Whitney opened several summer-only checkout stations in schools throughout the district. They were not permanent locations, but their existence called attention to the value of the summer initiative.

In addition to outreach at the Main Library, the revolution in youth services during Whitney's tenure extended to a dedicated children's reading room that opened

Top: Children reading at the Swinney Branch, E. F. Swinney school, 1915
Bottom: Swinney Branch, children's story hour, 1915

at the Westport Branch in late fall 1899. Young patrons and their guardians could choose from more than five thousand titles, from biographies to books on travel, history, science, literature, and fiction "specially selected for young people."

The aim extended beyond literacy and learning. In winter 1888, *The Star* reported on an unnamed fifteen-year-old boy who had read more than ninety-five books in three months. Among them were popular works by Mark Twain, James Fenimore Cooper, and Alexandre Dumas; classic rags-to-riches tales by Horatio Alger; and adventure stories by Elijah Kellogg. Stories were typically of the "the mildly exciting juvenile-type," the newspaper said, adding that the narratives were filled with "heroes [who] are rigidly moral and exemplary young lads, whose lives are lessons but who have a spice of boyish humanity about them." Authors—and the librarians who loaned their works—learned that youngsters would readily consume morality tales wrapped in exotic adventures.

Whitney and her staff continued to use the children's reading room to teach life lessons by making it a location of informal instruction. As just one early example, in June 1900, librarians stirred patriotic fervor in Kansas City's youth through a celebration of the anniversary of the United States' adoption of a national flag. "A great copy of the stars and stripes was unfurled, big enough to cover half of the children's reading room," *The Star* wrote. The lesson of the day was "the American flag, its origin, history, and destiny."

Washington Branch, with children studying at tables, 1920

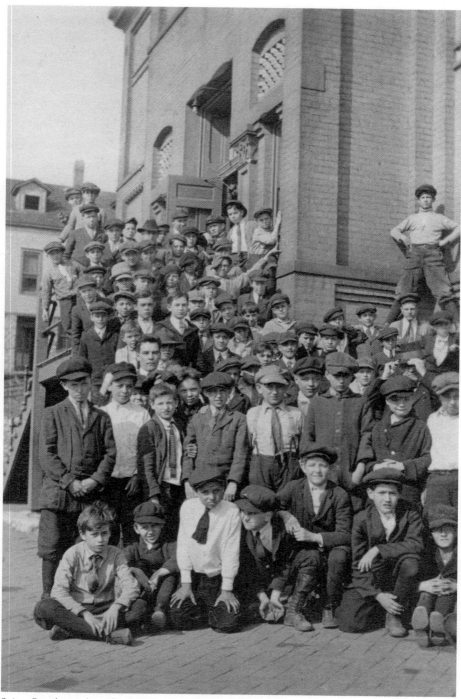

Switzer Branch, members of Boy's Club outside the front entrance, 1920

Under its next director, Purd Wright, the Library encouraged children's access to a broad spectrum of information. Wright recounted one anecdote about a boy who made his first visit in 1915 in search of a book that would show him how to throw a spitball, a popular (and now illegal) baseball pitch. The young patron, an eleven-year-old named Jimmy, indeed found what he wanted, but as Wright recalled, he also discovered there was valuable information on countless other topics at the Library. "What Jimmy learned at the library is not of so much importance," Wright later said, "as the fact that [now] he has the library habit. He has found that it can solve his problems. Jimmy is going to be well-educated."

The notion of a youthful "library habit" was surprisingly controversial in the early twentieth century. An article in *The Star* in 1910 lamented that local children were reading "trashy fiction" and warned that some youth "read . . . not wisely, but too much." The Library responded to the concerns by curating book lists for its first summer reading programs. Several librarians believed it was their duty to direct children toward the "right reading," not just what they wanted to read.

The Library would remain active in shaping literary tastes in the city. Recalling the story of the would-be spitball pitcher, Wright said that just as he had hoped, young Jimmy returned to the Library regularly to check out books on subjects beyond baseball, notably including the then-new science of wireless telegraphy. Wright continued to endorse lighter reading as an entrée to more substantial literature to boost learning. That included the placement of baseball posters in local schools with a listing of all the books in the Library on America's pastime. "We have books on every known game," he said to *The Star*. "We want every boy and girl to find that out."

The Library also encouraged children to enter its spaces through another innovative practice—story hours. On the first Saturday of March 1915, more than one hundred youngsters gathered in the Louis George Branch auditorium to hear librarian Elle Tough read a dramatic tale of the knights in the court of King Arthur. Tough understood that the story hours opened an entirely new pathway to learning about ideals and aspirations, and she structured each weekly selection around the concept that "the digestion of one truth opens the mind for the reception of another and more difficult one." Her Saturday sessions highlighted concepts like protection of the weak, the foolishness of discontent, and the impact of war on women living on the home front.

The Kansas City Public Library, *The Star* wrote, "learned long ago that it was not enough to build a library in a neighborhood and fill it with books." Effective library

Top: Children's Book Week, unidentified Kansas City Public Library location, 1923
Bottom: Swope Settlement Branch, 1920

services had to draw in the public. "Our story hours are advertisements for the books we have in the library," Tough said. "The children are told a story and then they want to know the name of the book and who wrote it. In that way they get into the habit of reading . . . books that build up character and become their life-long friends."

The joy of reading would not necessarily sell itself, however, and librarians came to understand that a less stringent framing of activities increased children's engagement

Top: Children's room, Main Library at Ninth and Locust, 1930
Bottom: Story hour attendees, East Branch entrance, 1938

with the Library and its programming. Nearly four decades after the first King Arthur story hour, it tapped into contemporary fascination with outer space and chose an interplanetary theme for its 1953 summer reading program. Vacationing students could enjoy "Reading by Rocket" by signing up and embarking on an imaginary interplanetary adventure. They enlisted as "cadets," with their schools as their "base stations" and grade levels as their "ranks." When participants finished a book, they moved from their base to a space station, then on to the moon, Venus, Mars, Jupiter, and Saturn before returning to Earth. Cadets who read sixteen books completed their trip around the galaxy and earned an astronaut's button as well as public acknowledgment on an honor roll printed on large sheets of construction paper cut to look like a spaceship.

These thematic programs illustrated just how heavily the Library was invested in children's services, its summer reading program, and their measurable student outcomes. In the summer of 1953, the editorial board of *The Star* commended the Library for selecting an outer-space reading theme that "coincide[s] with one of the most fascinating topics to the children today." In all of their youth programs, librarians now encouraged students to follow their interests and determine their own courses of study. The formal summer curriculum of recommended texts was replaced with a freedom to explore and investigate. This autonomy was celebrated in the 1950s, solidifying the turn from earlier concerns about students reading "trashy fiction." Now, when students explored their passions, self-directed study was understood as a virtue, not a cause for concern.

A FRUITFUL ASSOCIATION WITH SCHOOLS

The Library's longstanding relationship with the public school system allowed it to create several additional summer reading stations at elementary schools throughout the first half of the twentieth century. Building on Whitney's successes decades earlier, it opened fifteen more stations in summer 1945. Each operated just one day a week, but the schedule saw that at least one outpost was open daily, ensuring that students never lacked access to library materials.

Reaching youthful audiences meant dedicating systemwide resources and occasionally turning over the keys to the system to children's librarians. During the

Top: Children's story hour, children's room, Northeast Branch, 1950
Bottom: Children's room in the Southwest Branch, 1950

nationally observed Children's Book Week in 1949, for instance, public displays promoted reading materials with dolls and paper cutouts incorporating the slogan Make Friends with Books. Young readers learned about available books and then participated in contests to identify titles by their plots or characters. These displays gave greater exposure to the new juvenile releases in the Library system, with one branch going so far as to play recordings from popular Norwegian children's folktales by Gudrun Thorne-Thomsen.

Much of this outreach to community youth was formalized in 1944 with the creation of a new division, the Young People's Department. The name was borrowed from area churches looking to differentiate between the needs of younger children and the older kids now known as "teenagers." As it had done over its entire history, the Library worked to ensure the success of the outreach effort by adding expert subject-area librarians at each of its locations.

These new staff members faced many of the same challenges of inadequate space and budget as other librarians in the system. The Library was outgrowing—or already had outgrown—its facilities, particularly downtown. In an article in *The Star* in 1945, Director Harold Hamill maintained that if Kansas City was to develop the ideal modern library, it needed not only ample children's departments but also areas devoted to the social sciences, history, music, genealogy, fiction, business, and technical texts. Each subject area, it was believed, should have its own stacks and reading area. Few questioned the need to accommodate such wide-ranging, space-consuming fields as fiction and history, but making room for the materials in a youth department was a greater challenge. The then fifty-year-old Main Library, designed when reading space was kept to a minimum and books were stored in closed stacks, limited the ability to designate areas specifically for children.

Its location on the map was also problematic. With Kansas City expanding ever southward, the Library sat near the extreme northern edge of the city by 1950. This limited access for young people reliant on public transit to the urban core. Downtown also posed an image issue. At the midpoint of the century, the Main Library was near seven taverns—two directly across the street. Adjacency to libations may have been a perk for business professionals, but Library staffers saw it as a deterrent to youth and their parents.

"Developing the work of young people is greatly handicapped by the location of the library," Hamill told *The Star* in 1945. He believed that "many parents will not

Top: Central Branch, Central High School, ca. 1950s
Bottom: Children's room at the Northeast Branch, 1950

permit their children to come" to the Young People's Department. This lack of buy-in from families confounded the Library's hopes to "bridge the gap from the juvenile department to adult reading with special facilities for young people," *The Star* said.

The complications of access were mitigated by a healthy number of Library branches, but the nature of those locations and the legacy of Purd Wright's decision to place them in schools created its own problems. In 1945, all but three of the seventeen branches were in schools. Serving primarily as school libraries, they lacked the space to house materials for younger readers in individually themed areas complete with reading rooms. An obvious solution would have been the

Top: Children at the Main Library, 1955
Bottom: Paseo Branch, March 1957

construction of new facilities with greater space, but the school system could not offer funding for that while also meeting educational needs. By the time that Richard Sealock became director in 1950, the Library had seen several funding increases. They were not enough, however, to resolve its space deficiencies.

A solution finally took shape in 1956, when the school board proposed and voters passed the aforementioned $27 million bond issue authorizing construction of a new downtown Main Library and two large branches, one near the Plaza and the other in the city's less prosperous East Side neighborhood, at Linwood Boulevard and Tracy Avenue. This ambitious plan diverted from the existing model of placing branches in schools. But it would bolster the emphasis on programs and resources for youth. Notably, it promised to reward decades of work to meet the needs of Kansas City's diverse population as pressure mounted from under-resourced communities that had endured fragmented services for decades.

As the Library embraced its larger budget, children's spaces expanded across the system. Jean Merrill, the director of children's services, penned a holiday column in *The Star* in December 1963. "Christmas," she wrote, "is a time for giving special books to special children, books that will be read and re-read, cherished through the years, and finally passed along to another generation." Top recommendations for that

Patrons entering the children's library, Main Library at Twelfth and McGee, 1960

year included *Mother Goose and Nursery Rhymes* by Philip Reed, *The Wild Swans* by Hans Christian Andersen, and *The Turret* by Margery Sharp. The first two were new printings of classic tales, but the endorsement of *The Turret* drew attention to a newer work that was part of Sharp's *The Rescuers* series. These referrals served to highlight the Library's role as an authority on children's reading for the community.

THE LONG DRIFT APART

The Library's outreach to children and its relationship to the city's public school system was not without concern or debate. Predictably, money was paramount. Library director Louis Nourse, hired in 1939, was repeatedly frustrated with the school board, seeing the Library as underappreciated and underfunded.

Libraries under the supervision of boards of education were common in the late nineteenth and early twentieth centuries, but by the early 1940s, Indianapolis was the only other comparably sized city that did not have an independent library board. This had direct financial consequences. The American Library Association recommended a funding target of one dollar per capita for all municipal libraries, but Kansas City, with a library system offering more than the usual menu of services, operated on a budget of just seventy-five cents per person.

Pressure to expand library services mounted as the population of Kansas City expanded. Between 1925 and 1941, the number of juvenile patrons grew nearly 60 percent, from over 50,000 to almost 80,000. At the same time, adult users doubled to 106,000. For a system with branches in schools and a board that placed an emphasis on serving students, there was increasing demand to serve more of the city, even as resources tightened. The passage of the $27 million bond issue was still a decade and a half away.

The Library became a target for funding reductions in the early 1940s due to the economic strains on the school district. A growing number of Kansas Citians wondered why it drew from tax revenues assigned to the school when state legislation already allowed cities to collect library-specific taxes. Library supporters proposed a plan to separate the institutions, maintaining the board of education's tax levies while also supporting the Library with funds available from proposed municipal levies. The push to separate from the schools had broad support from parent-teacher organizations and civic groups interested in increasing school quality for the fifty-five thousand children in the district. Support also came from the Urban League, the University Women's Club, and parent-teacher associations from fifteen schools within the district.

In November 1941, Nourse made his concerns public in a speech delivered to the Citizens' Public Schools organization at Kansas City's downtown Municipal Auditorium. After detailing the value of the Library to schoolchildren and adults alike, he ended his talk with an indignant "nobody gives a damn about the library." Critics, like schools superintendent Harold Hunt, had recently called the Library a "severe drain," saying it pulled $300,000 a year from the district's budget. Nourse countered that for nearly seventy years, tax revenues had been jointly earmarked for the school district and public library, and it was misleading to suggest that the school district would simply save all of that money if the Library became the responsibility of the city. While some advocated for the closure of kindergartens and the library system as cost-saving measures, Nourse tried to articulate the low-cost contributions of the Library to the wider community.

In his defense of the Library, Nourse explained that schools still would have to pay at least $90,000 a year for school library services. Additionally, he reasoned, the cost to the community to replace the other system libraries would be very high. "The cost of fifteen branch libraries alone would be $2 million if built by the municipality," he said. "They cost practically nothing when they are built into high schools." He then contrasted the local situation with that of libraries in St. Louis, which were maintained under statutes that allowed the city council to spend 40 percent of a property tax mill on library services. True, Nourse admitted, the amount a similar tax would generate in Kansas City—just over $200,000 a year—was a third lower than the existing allocation, and municipal funding under state statute did not actually meet the needs of the St. Louis system. They "can't even afford a gallon of paint for maintenance," he noted dryly.

Following his remarks, *The Star* published an article detailing widespread public support for Nourse's comments. The newspaper reported that he was feeling "sheepish" about swearing but did not apologize and only wished he had remembered to mention the overdue fees—more than $1,000 a month—that the Library turned over to the schools' general budget. A little less than a year later, in October 1942, Nourse submitted his resignation, leaving to become assistant librarian of the St. Louis Public

Library. His new position was a step down in pay, and it seemed clear that he was looking to end his conflict with the school district and seek out new opportunities.

The Kansas City school board briefly considered a proposal to eliminate the head librarian position and return management of the Library to the superintendent. On November 25, 1942, more than sixty residents packed a board meeting and erupted into raucous applause when the body decided to maintain separate Library governance. Priscilla Burd took over as interim director, briefly becoming the Library's third female leader before being replaced less than five months later by Harold Hamill in May 1943.

A new director did not bring the desired stability, and throughout much of the 1940s, the Library's administration continued to struggle with the school board. In one dramatic example, the board met in midsummer 1947 to renew the appointments of Library employees—normally a formality. In a surprisingly short, thirty-minute session, the board voted 5–1 to reappoint the entire staff except for Hamill and Dorothea Hyle, the chief of circulation. As their appointments were to end the following week, they were automatically "released" from their duties without formal termination.

Tensions had built for years as the board accused Hamill of exceeding his budget by $25,000 annually and, allegedly, raising his own salary by $1,000, to $7,500. He had nearly lost his appointment a year earlier, but the president of the board, Butler Disman, a Hamill supporter, said the salary increase had been decided by a board committee, not by Hamill. Further, as Disman explained, Hamill's salary was still short of the American Library Association's recommended $8,500 for a system the size of Kansas City. Hamill responded to the charges against him by reminding the board that, despite being the director, he was not granted full access to information about Library expenditures and revenues nor control over the Library's budget. Nor, for that matter, did Hamill have authority over any kind of expenses charged to the Library, so he could not have altered his own salary.

CONSTITUTIONAL PROTECTION

During the same years that Kansas City was debating matters of money, schools, and libraries, library funding had also become part of a statewide discussion. In response to questions about municipal support for library services, a special state constitutional convention was called to seek innovative solutions. Library advocates lobbied for an amendment assuring fiscal support for public libraries, deeming them critical to the state's educational infrastructure. Louis Nourse, still working for the St. Louis library system, and Harold Hamill were especially outspoken over two years of deliberations. Hamill, also representing the Missouri Library Association as its president, canvassed the state to promote the proposed library amendment. In a special election on February 27, 1945, voters gave it 63 percent approval, making Missouri one of only three states—alongside Michigan and Arkansas—with constitutional provisions for public libraries.

Article IX, Section 10 of Missouri's state constitution read:

It is hereby declared to be the policy of the state to promote the establishment and development of free public libraries and to accept the obligation of their support by the state and its subdivisions and municipalities in such a manner as may be provided by law. When any such subdivision or municipality supports a free library, the general assembly shall grant aid to such public library in such manner and in such amounts as may be provided by law.

Additional legislation that same year was proposed to create a separate Kansas City Public Library district for taxation, with boundaries matching those of the school district. It called for a board with six members (three appointed by the mayor and three by the board of education), a one-mill property tax (one dollar per $1,000 of assessed value), and authorization for the Library to borrow money for buildings. The idea of a new taxing district drew opposition from several business leaders, however, and the new law provided a compromise. It did not remove the Library from the school district's jurisdiction. Although addressing school and Library funding concerns, including a boost in annual Library revenues from $300,000 to more than $425,000, the measure effectively delayed full independence for the Kansas City Public Library for another forty years.

DEPARTURE OF HAMILL AND HYLE

On February 20, 1947, the board drew up a resolution to formally separate the Library's expenditures from those of the school district—seen widely as a move toward cutting district funding of the Library. The measure also included a controversial proviso: The head librarian was prohibited from "releasing information to the public" without prior approval from the school board. Without any apparent limits on the scope of forbidden "information," *The Star* and *The Times* began referring to Hamill as "Kansas City's muzzled librarian," and the Library suspended publicity releases, public reports, new books lists, and a popular radio broadcast. In the face of heavy criticism, the prohibition lasted only about a month, but as described in *The Star*, relations between the Library and the school board deteriorated to a point of total dysfunction from which Hamill and Hyle could not recover.

Upon receiving word of his "release" while attending the American Library Association's annual conference in San Francisco, Hamill informed the ALA of the circumstances. According to *The Star*, the organization already viewed the librarian position at the Kansas City Public Library as "questionable"; it was unclear who could be recruited to the job now. Hamill, meanwhile, with his reputation undiminished, landed on his feet as director of the Los Angeles Public Library—then the third-largest public system in the nation—at twice his former salary in Kansas City.

Complicating matters in Kansas City, the actions of rank-and-file staff members made their opposition to the board's handling of Library matters clear. Katherine McNabb, head of the cataloguing department, resigned in protest. *The Star* reported at least twenty-one additional resignations, including those of the librarian and children's librarian at the Jewish Community Center Branch and a professional library assistant at the East Branch. Earlier, 133 of the Library's 134 employees had signed a petition supporting the reappointment of Hamill.

No official explanation was given for the dismissal of Dorothea Hyle, but it likely was related to the board's moratorium on communication with the public. In her final year at the Library, she created a popular radio program, *The Voice of the Library*, that was canceled in the midst of the imbroglio. The five-minute show had been broadcast both locally and nationally.

A graduate of Westport High School, Hyle had attended Ward-Belmont College in Nashville, the University of Missouri, the University of Kansas, and Columbia

University's library school, one of the best in the nation. After her dismissal in Kansas City, she directed the Harrisonville library in Cass County. Her work there led to her appointment by the US State Department in 1951 to be the American vice-consul in Barcelona, Spain, and director of the agency's library there. So strong was her leadership that Hyle was profiled in the *Christian Science Monitor* and other national media outlets.

After the departures of Hamill and Hyle, Harry Brinton, head of the Library's acquisitions department, was appointed acting librarian. Some sentiment remained to transfer management of the system to the city government as ongoing divisiveness made significant changes or even day-to-day management difficult. Shortly after his appointment, Brinton reported to the school board that "the library is unable to obtain qualified personnel," and hours and services were curtailed. For two years, local publications continued to report on school board members squabbling over procedures for hiring a new permanent librarian. At the same time, citizens' groups continued to call for the transfer of library governance to the city.

AN UNPLANNED EXPERIMENT

School districts' subsidization of public libraries once had been common across the country, but the Kansas City experience was notable for the longevity of the practice and became an inadvertent experiment in library management practices. It yielded short-term economic benefits, but by the 1980s, many of the most outspoken stakeholders had come to believe that the long-term costs to effective librarianship far outweighed any economic savings. Still, untangling the Library from the school system was no easy task.

There had been several failed attempts at separation already. The *Library Journal* identified at least six efforts, including two sustained campaigns, the first in the late 1940s and the second in the early '70s. They tended to parallel economic downturns, suggesting that financial pressures were a motivation. Despite the dysfunction cited locally, Kansas City in the early 1980s had become a tempting archetype for some cities that sought to save money by combining services and reducing overhead—"an interesting case study," library researcher Susan Spaeth Cherry said. In truth, as Cherry and others argued, the setup served as a cautionary tale about a combined approach to library management.

In her 1982 study published in *American Libraries* magazine, Cherry noted that shared management worked best in cities of five thousand people or fewer. Those smaller communities were more likely to save scarce resources and increase patron outreach. In Kansas City in the 1940s, when serious conversations about Library separation began, the population hovered around four hundred thousand. By the late '70s, it was five hundred thousand.

The awkwardness of the schools-libraries relationship was well understood on both sides. Director Harold Jenkins told a library publication in 1982 that "the system isn't something I'd put my name on." He concluded, "We try to make the best of a situation that has been here for many years." Schools superintendent Robert Wheeler agreed: "I don't think it's the best arrangement."

Mary Arney was a library-championing member of the school board at the time—but also an exception. Looking back in 2023, she said the Library was a secondary concern for the majority of the board members. "Mr. Jenkins would get maybe ten minutes at the end of a board meeting to get passed whatever he could get passed. That was it," she said. "At one point," Arney recalled, "a group came and said they'd like to be Friends of the Library (serving as a volunteer support organization). The board said, 'No, we don't want any Friends of the Library. *We* run this.' The Friends, of course, would have nothing to do with running it. But you couldn't explain it to them."

The Library's status as an independent taxing district saved it from the worst of the funding cuts, but the school district was struggling with declining enrollment and stagnant revenues. Voters' approval of two new levy measures signaled their esteem for the system; still, the Library spent much of the 1970s cutting staff and services.

It would take a series of jolts—a long and winding landmark legal case, a new Library leader with an innovative approach to dispensing Library services, and action by state legislators—to finally effect a breakup. In 1977, in *Missouri v. Jenkins*, the Kansas City school district and the children of two of its board members sued the state of Missouri and surrounding suburban school districts, claiming that they were responsible for alleviating the harm caused by white migration to the suburbs. The litigation's prospects were uncertain given the district's untested legal strategies, and for more than eighteen years, the case wound through the District Court of Western Missouri, the US Court of Appeals for the Eighth Circuit, and the US Supreme Court, which ruled 5–4 against the district in 1995. While significant in local and legal circles, the

Library Director Daniel J. Bradbury seated at desk

importance of the case to the Library had less to do with that outcome than with the added uncertainty it cast on the future of the school district.

Missouri v. Jenkins was six years into its legal odyssey when, in 1983, Daniel J. Bradbury took the helm of a Library system fraught by tenuous finances, aging branches, and its uncomfortable position as a vassal to the school district. A graduate of the University of Missouri-Kansas City, he had worked for the Rolling Hills Consolidated Library District in northwest Missouri and most recently as head of the Janesville (Wisconsin) Public Library and Recreation District. Arney, who served on the Kansas City school board from 1980 to 1988, pushed hard for his hiring: "I said, 'This is the guy we want.'"

Colleagues of the thirty-seven-year-old described him as levelheaded, detail oriented, and financially savvy. Speaking to *The Star*, Bradbury expressed concern about the "very austere" financial situation in Kansas City. Staff contraction and other budget tightening could not continue, he said, and he set a course to "branch out" and develop new revenue streams. "It seems like there's a lot of effort, enthusiasm, and interest in rekindling urban excitement," he told the newspaper. "I would hope that we could participate . . . in that rebirth, growth and provide a level of library services that matches that excitement."

LIBRARY INDEPENDENCE

His first order of business, Bradbury now recalls, was to assess and replace branches. New locations began opening on a regular basis. There was no mandate to separate the Library from the school district—and really, no serious discussion of splitting. But with the attention of the school board diverted to the desegregation case and away from Library management issues, Bradbury saw it as the "right place and right time" to pursue independence. He believed an independent Library would allow him to "wipe the slate clean" of the old branches in schools, which was particularly important at a time of peak interest in service to the entire community on a more equitable basis.

Bradbury's attention dovetailed with an internal study, released in late 1984, that made a case for closing or consolidating thirteen of the Library's fourteen branches, leaving only the Plaza location untouched. Most of the targeted facilities were in schools, with a few others in shopping centers or serving as smaller, stand-alone sites that did not provide full services. A tax levy increase in 1986 provided much-needed revenue to begin the reorganization. "Dan had a plan for how the money would be used, [for] what was needed," Arney said. "He equitably set up neighborhood libraries . . . made sure there was one here, one there, and one over there. He's very intelligent, and he could persuade people."

The latter attribute would prove useful in the push for a conclusion to the now four-decade struggle to detach the Library from the school system. The school board came to accept the idea of a separate Library and instructed the district's lobbyist to assist Bradbury in crafting state legislation authorizing the establishment of urban library districts in Missouri. It was submitted and passed in a short two years.

Children's section, looking to the northeast, with the children's information desk in view, original Plaza Branch, 2001

The urban district classification allowed the Library to maintain its existing tax district boundaries, ensure uniform taxation across that service area, and—no less important—head off alternate proposals for change, such as consolidation with the Mid-Continent Public Library. In 1988, voters in the Kansas City school district approved the creation of an urban library district and separately approved (as required by law) the transfer of the Library's portion of the mill levy from the school to the newly independent taxing authority, the Kansas City Public Library. Arney, who once had chaired the school board's library committee, was named president pro tempore of the first Library board in December 1988. She remained its head until 1990. With this autonomy, the Library was positioned to continue its traditionally excellent youth services, reach out more effectively into the community, and enter a golden, twenty-first-century era of innovation in librarianship and service to Kansas City.

5

INNOVATIVE LIBRARIANSHIP

*We need a place of center where we can rub shoulders with
the wisdom and heritage of previous generations, to raise
the level of dignity and decency in the world.*

**—DST REALTY CHAIRMAN AND LIBRARY CHAMPION
PHIL KIRK**

In 1917, head librarian Purd Wright told *The Moving Picture World*, a film industry trade journal, that "the presentation on the motion screen of a well-known book creates an instant demand on public libraries for the book itself, and so long as only worthy books are shown libraries benefit." Even at that early date, as US involvement in World War I loomed, Wright recognized the challenges faced by libraries because of new media. His comment highlighted the multiple ways that libraries could adapt to modern technologies and use them to enhance literary culture while serving the public on its own terms. Beyond making services more efficient or expansive, these advances in technology transformed the nature of libraries, turning them into indispensable centers of culture and places of empowerment. At each turn, the Kansas City Public Library proved eager to embrace changing circumstances and introduce its own innovations into practice.

TECHNOLOGY BOOSTS THE LIBRARY

Only a few years after Carrie Westlake Whitney introduced one of the nation's earliest public library children's rooms, and as Kansas Citians were still getting used to the Dewey decimal system, the Library considered how sound recordings, motion pictures, and radio might affect librarianship. Wright was not alone in seeing the potential for movies to enhance literary culture, but other librarians feared that the film and other new media and entertainment industries would threaten literature's popularity and the utilization of public libraries.

Reflecting on his career decades later in 1937, Wright admitted that the effect of film and radio on libraries had been more complex than he originally predicted.

Art and music department reference desk, Main Library at Ninth and Locust Streets, 1955

Initially, phonographs, or "sound reproduction," simply brought entertainment into people's homes. The enhanced access to music meant that among library patrons, "a desire was created to know about it, its composer, and all else," as Wright noted. The mass production of automobiles similarly threatened to divert leisure time from reading to other pursuits, but it also stimulated a demand for books about maintenance and travel. Likewise, the popularity of moving pictures and radio created demand for books about the technology and business models underpinning those media. Walt Disney was not the only Kansas City Public Library patron searching for this knowledge.

Technology could improve accessibility, circulation, and efficiency, as Wright had discovered in allowing patrons to renew books by telephone starting in 1913. New options for communication facilitated operations and expanded the nature of services offered to the community. In the World War I era, Wright expressed pride that long-distance phones were installed in the Library for use by patrons. Traveling soldiers, especially, made use of a new "writing room" that held an oak table and six chairs. In this case, the timeless tradition of handwritten letters met a new community need and became, once again in Wright's words, "an innovation in library buildings."

Wright did acknowledge challenges introduced by rapidly changing technology. "The most real of library problems, probably because of their proximity and a lack of prophetic ability, is the photographic reproduction on the screen . . . and the radio," he surmised. "What will happen in the educational world, and especially in that branch of it called the public library, depends all but wholly upon the clarity of judgment of those in charge, and available resources." He did not elaborate, but it seems clear that Wright was questioning the educational merit of content being produced for popular media—the plots and subject matter were hardly confined to what he considered "worthy books."

Even early in the century, Wright foresaw difficulties for librarians who utilized emerging technologies. Unintended consequences, such as budgeting for a reduction in late fees because patrons could now conveniently renew their book loans by phone, had to be considered. Other ideas simply did not work due to cost, logistics, or other factors. For example, the Library experimented with lending books through parcel post, sending them directly to patrons' homes and then facilitating returns to post office branches using preprinted labels. Wright came to believe the service wasn't being utilized by the public because of the trips required to the post office, and he hoped that mail carriers would eventually collect returned books from individual residences.

Wright's observations presaged developments of a much later era when many wondered if the internet and e-books might displace physical libraries. But in his time, as now, the public library proved its agility and relevance by diversifying community services. In one instance, in early 1914, the Starr Piano Company donated 480

Library employee working in the bindery, Main Library, ca. 1940s

Two unidentified adults using microfilm readers, Main Library, 1955

player piano music rolls. Player pianos hardly qualify as cutting-edge technology today, but more than a century ago, these new instruments prompted an expansion of tech services and outreach by the Library. Additionally, Wright said, "it is a most effective way not only of combating shoddy music, but of cultivating a taste for music worthwhile."

The Kansas City Public Library reached still wider audiences through radio programming. In October 1937, the *Bulletin of the American Library Association* identified it as one of eight libraries nationally that hosted regular broadcast programs for children. The segments involved storytelling, reviews of children's books, and author interviews. In the early 1940s, Dorothea F. Hyle, then director of public relations, organized a broadcast series, *Civic Forum: Getting Acquainted with Your Public Library*, on radio station KCMO. Episodes aired for twenty minutes on the second Saturday morning of the month and garnered national attention in the library sphere. Later, Hyle's *The Voice of the Library* series won the American Library Association's John Cotton Dana Award for excellence in public relations.

Top: A presentation with motion picture projector, Main Library, ca. 1950

Bottom: Two employees seated at the film department reference desk, Main Library, ca. 1955

Radio programs gave the Library a chance to publicize the many innovations of the time. Director Harold Hamill described the necessity of broadcasts in the modern era: "It isn't going to do the library or anyone else any good to collect carefully and have on hand needed material if there is no demand made upon our collection. It is our business to inform the public of what our resources are so that the public may make use of these materials." Broadcasts took note of Library resources for returning war veterans, consisting of publications about the challenges they encountered, career and training information, reading-for-enrichment materials, and referrals to veterans' agencies.

One program discussed the possibility that the new Main Library building that Hamill had recently proposed might also serve as a public memorial to World War II. Mae Reed Porter, president of the Friends of the Kansas City Public Library group founded in 1938, shared that vision, saying there could be "no finer tribute to our war dead than the erection of a living, human institution such as a public library; a place where the doors stand open to every class and color; a truly democratic institution which embodies the principles of a better way of life for which our soldiers died."

Other broadcasts, often lighter in tone, included staff banter and even the impersonation of a book as it was going through the bindery department (as did more than sixteen thousand titles a year) or a microfilm machine. Such segments featured conversations about the inner workings of the Library, with staff describing how the still-unusual bindery and the newer microfilm machines increased efficiency and cut costs.

By the 1940s, telephones had become an increasingly popular part of reference services. Patrons could call the Library with questions that ranged from the practical, such as how to make applesauce, to the trivial, like the middle initial of the sitting governor. Whether by telephone or in-person outreach, an informal library philosophy emerged: The Library goes to the reader. The Library placed special collection boxes in areas around the city where librarians believed they could be of use to professionals: hospitals, factories, and businesses including North American Aviation, Hall Brothers, and Kansas City Power and Light. Additionally, it delivered more than four hundred thousand books annually to the city's public schools. It is no wonder that in 1944, a staggering 46 percent of the city's population held a library card—the highest among large cities across the nation—and patrons checked out some two million books.

Top: The Library's original Bookmobile, 1950

Bottom: Interior of the original Bookmobile, with Lois Payne, assistant at the Lincoln Branch, 1954

The Kansas Citian, a Chamber of Commerce newsletter, described the public library as "probably the greatest single cultural influence in Kansas City."

Technology enabled the Library to reach its patrons more directly with a bookmobile. In 1950, after years of planning, the system purchased what it called a "branch library on wheels" to deliver materials to homes, schools, and other locations across the metropolitan area. It would quickly surpass physical branches in circulation—more than one hundred thousand books loaned in its first year alone, compared to the branch average of more than thirty thousand. That service continued to meet patrons at convenient locations through the early 1960s, when a new Main Library with plentiful parking drew more patrons downtown.

In a similar mobility effort in 1969, two local teachers joined Penny Northern (the head of the Library's film department) in touring Instant Movies at the Curbstone around the city. With a rented eighteen-foot van, power generator, and film projector, they screened educational clips to nearly ten thousand children in different residential areas over ten weeks.

A "SPACE AGE" HOME

The most visible change for the Library in this period was the July 1960 opening of the new $4.5 million Main Library at Twelfth and Oak Streets, a modern structure capable of meeting twentieth-century expectations. Over the previous decade, circulation had increased from 1.9 million volumes to more than 3.8 million annually, which pointed to the need for a new facility to accommodate such growth and position the Library for the future.

The old building could no longer be expanded to meet the public's rising demands or house the Library's growing collection, much less serve as an effective hub for the branch system and school district. Modern Library patrons expected such creature comforts as air conditioning, while Library administrators needed flexibility to adapt spaces for ever-changing technologies and standards. Interstate highways and automobiles steadily displaced streetcars and other forms of public transportation, yet the old Locust Street location lacked sufficient space for expanded parking. Limited floor space there meant that the school district offices sprawled out across several locations.

Top: Looking south through the first-floor lobby, Main Library at Twelfth and McGee Streets, 1960
Bottom: Looking northeast from the second floor, Main Library, 1960

Working with head architect Edward W. Tanner, Library leaders articulated a vision of a modern, functional space. The new building caused an immediate sensation, and circulation jumped more than 50 percent in the first six months of operation. A limestone-clad, two-level garage addressed the need for parking, and the structure was surrounded by the downtown "loop" of interstate highways, close to retail, public transportation, and local government facilities. The Library occupied about 165,000 square feet on five levels and additional storage and office space on two basement levels. The Renaissance Revival architecture of the old building had long fallen out of favor and was now supplanted by modern lines accentuated by curtain-wall aluminum and glass. Glazed metal partitions or bookcases separated departments on each floor and were designed to be reconfigurable as Library trends shifted. As described in *The Star* during construction in 1957, "A unique feature of the building will be flexibility. The only permanent walls will be around stairways, elevators and other areas required by the building codes." From a television studio in the building, the school district broadcast 4½ hours of self-produced educational programming daily.

Framed reproductions area of the art and music department, third floor, Main Library, 1960

Top: Arthur Kraft mosaic near the entrance to the children's library, Main Library

Bottom: Children's story hour room, Main Library, architects Edward W. Tanner & Associates. Recognized by the Kansas City Chapter of the American Institute of Architects, 1960

The Library had transformed since the days when it housed the city's arts and sciences museums, but its mission continued to emphasize the cultural uplift of children and families. This commitment could be seen in the seventeen thousand art reproductions that became part of the circulating collection by the mid-1970s and were available for checkout for up to two months. The new children's department, opened in 1960, could be accessed through a separate entrance where visitors were greeted by a circus-themed mosaic tile mural designed by local artist Arthur Kraft, who described it as "an invitation to the child to enter into the fanciful land of an enchanted forest where all things are possible, as they are in the imagination of all children."

Modern art influences extended further into the Main Library, with a curved pattern in the terrazzo floor echoing the main entrance's curve and a ceramic tile mosaic by local artist Gabriella Polony Mountain. Metal screens diffused recessed light from the ceiling, and reflecting the times, birch panels covered the west wall of the foyer while vinyl tile covered most of the concrete floors.

The mid-century embrace of modernism, however dynamic, did depart from the past in at least one regrettable way. As librarians shuttled thousands of books out of the old Locust Street building, they left behind several objects and decorations that had long graced the walls and inspired the masses. The most unfortunate loss was a painting by renowned muralist Edwin Howland Blashfield. Commissioned for $20,000 and donated to the Library by the Kansas City chapter of the Daughters of the American Revolution in 1918, *The Call of Missouri* featured a woman, who represented the state, observing her sons leaving for war.

The piece remained in its prominent place above a fireplace after the US Trade School purchased the building, and visitors reported seeing it as late as 1979. But by the time the Ozark National Life Insurance Company bought the building at auction in 1984, the painting had disappeared. It finally resurfaced in 2013 at a Dallas art gallery, which was selling it for an anonymous client. The then Library director R. Crosby Kemper III sought legal counsel to determine whether the Library could still claim ownership, to no avail. The following year, the painting was sold for $149,000.

Most of the Library's pursuits of modernity proved more enduring. When the first Plaza Branch opened in 1967, Missouri State Librarian Charles O'Halloran described it as "a commitment to human enlightenment." Its significance was better characterized in a staff newsletter as "a successful venture in total community library service."

Original Plaza Branch, Ward Parkway and Main Streets

The branch's collection did not aim to be comprehensive or to serve student researchers but instead catered to city residents who wanted to learn about everyday interests such as gardening, cooking, or crafting. Its location, adjacent to residential areas and the city's most popular suburban shopping district, was conducive to a unique programming menu that included paper recycling, children's story time and theater sessions, voter education drives, tax aid, a post office station, and gathering spaces for vocational groups. Architects designed the building to accommodate one hundred thousand books.

The Plaza Branch's most memorable architectural flourish set the tone for a literary collection that emphasized gardening and other popular hobbies. It could be seen along the north side of the building, where a wall of glass permitted natural illumination of a hanging garden extending from ground level to the ceiling of the two-story library. Designers touted the increased humidity that they believed would benefit plants and books alike. A fifteen-foot transparent water column and three water domes completed the effect. In its convenient location, the facility effectively served the community for the remainder of the century.

MISSOURI VALLEY SPECIAL COLLECTIONS

On December 1, 1960, the new Main Library opened a dedicated space, the Missouri Valley Room, where visitors could research the history of their families and the geographic region using archival material. The concept was in keeping with the Library's original approach of dividing services into thematic departments: education, philosophy, and religion; literature; popular library; history, travel, and biography; business and technical; social science; art and music; film; and children's.

That specialization extended to hiring practices, which added subject experts to the staff roster. Katherine Goldsmith, for example, worked as a historian, teacher, and author before joining the Missouri Valley Room during the 1960s. She became a significant contributor to the History of Kansas City Project under sociologist and historian A. Theodore Brown of the University of Kansas City. Goldsmith's work resulted in numerous publications, and patrons can still access her research materials in collections across several regional repositories. Peggy Smith, a staff member who worked in the Missouri Valley Room between 1960 and her retirement in 1985, contributed to multiple publications and was credited with the renaming of the Inter-City Viaduct between the two Kansas Cities to the Lewis and Clark Viaduct.

From its 1960 opening to its current iteration, the Missouri Valley Room has provided Kansas City's residents with a free and open historical and genealogical research capacity that is unusual among public libraries. Its name was inspired by the Missouri Valley Historical Society, which started meeting in the Westport Branch earlier in the century. The airy third-floor reading room with a two-story ceiling was flanked by a mezzanine and a sixty-foot-wide Daniel MacMorris mural depicting historical people and events along the watershed of the Missouri River Valley, from sixteenth-century Spanish explorer Hernando de Soto to depictions of science and engineering in the mid-twentieth century. The room opened with collections that the Library had accumulated over the years but were previously scattered among different departments or locked away due to concerns over preservation, security, or space. "For the first time, we're bringing out many of the items of the collection into a suitable atmosphere for the kind of historical research for which they were intended," said then director Richard Sealock.

These materials included some ten thousand reference volumes, vertical files, maps, scrapbooks, microfilm, photographs, newspaper clippings, and indexes on various subjects of regional significance. A donation from the Native Sons of Kansas City, Missouri, spanned the region's culture and commerce during the era of westward expansion in the nineteenth century, with such noteworthy items as the personal papers of Robert T. Van Horn, a city founder and *Kansas City Journal* editor. The Western History Collection held a trove of maps, early publications by scientific explorer John Wesley Powell, and materials covering explorers, fur traders, homesteaders, and the cattle trade. Genealogy resources included a collection donated in the 1930s by lumber baron John Barber White (who served as president of the Missouri Valley Historical Society from 1912 to 1923), and the Library hosted the Heart of America Genealogical Society collections and activities.

The Missouri Valley Room's city directories, dating to 1859, remain a powerful tool in researching the lives and business activities of ancestors or historical figures. The Library purchased a ten-thousand-piece collection from the estate of Brookings Montgomery, a local photographer, that captured images of Kansas City from the 1890s to the 1950s and formed the basis of a growing photograph collection. Librarians meticulously clipped and indexed local newspapers by subject headings since 1900, sparing students and researchers the painstaking work of

Missouri Valley Room and Daniel MacMorris mural, 1960

skimming "each issue, each edition, from front page to last, to locate your information." Providing a guide to the Missouri Valley Special Collections is the Local History Index, which is now searchable on KChistory.org and comprises thirty-eight thousand entries.

CUSP OF THE INTERNET AGE

In 1975, *Kansas City Magazine* published an article about "Kansas City's Brain," which it said "is over one hundred years old but unlike most brains . . . is growing larger and quicker with age." It referenced the Library's new use of computers to catalog its collections and to facilitate access to its first online database, the *New York Times* Information Bank. The Kansas City Public Library was just the fifth public library in the nation to subscribe to the *Times*'s service, joining the rarified company of institutions such as the Associated Press, the NBC television network, and the United Nations.

In describing how hundreds of thousands of records could be searched in mere minutes using a computer terminal, Library advocates boasted, "The move is toward the full knowledge center." The service provided up to twenty-five hours of online access to abstracts of *New York Times* articles published after 1969 and abstracts from sixty-five non-*Times* publications, including *Time, Fortune, Jet, Washington Post, Christian Science Monitor*, and the *Los Angeles Times* from 1972 onward.

Dorothy Arneson, who oversaw the program for the Kansas City Public Library, explained how it would better serve the community. Staff used the technology to answer patron questions and to help with research projects. Where it had once taken four or five months for the printed *Times Index* to be updated and issued, the database could now provide library access to stories within five days of their publication. Staff members could then access abstracts via the computer and direct patrons to microfiche copies of the full articles, which would be available within two weeks of the original publication date.

Director Harold Jenkins recognized that a new era had dawned with "the move . . . toward instant information" and "a new breed of librarians more properly called information scientists and specialists." He added, "There are no rules and only one guiding principal . . . reach the people." By then, it was also possible for the Library to transmit short documents by "telecopier," or fax machine. With that technology, it could instantly communicate in printed format with institutions around the city, even "accommodating prisoners in the county jail."

The many economic challenges of the 1970s introduced difficulties in balancing ever-increasing building costs and declining staff numbers with the desire and need to become a comprehensive technological information center. Nevertheless, the Library advanced its role in the community under the leadership of Stephen Kirk and Harold Jenkins in the late 1960s, '70s, and early '80s. The Library accumulated 9,000 phonograph records, 1,400 films, 700 US phone directories, 300 foreign directories, county maps covering the entire nation, special files for over 2,000 Kansas City organizations and foundations, 413,000 government documents, a computerized catalog, a braille books collection, photocopiers for patron use (at ten cents per page), and books on tape. It added formal bibliographic services for school classrooms.

The reference department fielded more than 650 phone inquiries daily, and a separate legislative hotline answered questions for those following state and national politics. Although language translation was not a formal service, some Library staff members were fluent in Spanish, Chinese, Greek, Latin, or German and could translate passages if needed, such as when patrons brought in their German beer steins. In other cases, people came in seeking help with personal problems, and Library staff routinely referred them to social service agencies.

Important as these advances and services were, the era of persistent "stagflation" took an economic toll. Upon announcing his retirement as director in 1982, Harold Jenkins lamented losing the equivalent of 110 full-time jobs over the previous nine years: "As always, we're paring back, paring back. Get rid of the fat and cut into the lean." William H. Hoffman, author of an illustrated history of the Library on its one hundredth anniversary, concluded the volume with foresight into the impending information age: "The proliferation of the community's needs in the years ahead will demand new types of services as well as the revitalization of old ones."

Balancing patron expectations for modern library technology against a shrinking budget fell to a new director, Daniel J. Bradbury. It was during his tenure that the Library embraced the internet age while securing two tax levy increases and crafting an identity independent of the school district. The Library's financial situation and standards of service were also bolstered by the reconstitution of the Friends of the Library support organization in 1984 and establishment of an endowment fund.

Staffing levels, and consequently open business hours, were gradually restored to keep locations open in the evenings, on Saturdays, and even on Sundays. These developments allowed the Library to blaze a path in technology and community programming, situating it for excellence in the twenty-first century.

Early in Bradbury's tenure, a most unlikely figure buoyed the Library with a notable donation. David A. Taggart, described in *The Kansas City Times* as a man who "lived a pauper but died a philanthropist," had become a devoted library booster even though he'd never held a library card. An army veteran of the European theater in World War II, Taggart spent the latter years of his life as a loner, living in an eighty-dollar-a-month rented room and keeping his tattered clothes together with safety pins. Among his few possessions were some pens, a shaving kit, and several books on philosophy—the latter described as "pretty heavy stuff" by one of the executors of his estate. By living humbly, he managed to save around $43,000 by the time of his death on November 27, 1983. After some months of probate proceedings and subtracting final expenses, his will left $40,000 to the Library (the equivalent of more than $100,000 in 2023), which was used to start an endowment fund for book purchases.

In 1985, Bradbury reached a reciprocal lending agreement with the Mid-Continent Public Library and other neighboring metropolitan library systems—a partnership that had eluded them since the 1960s. Anyone living in the Kansas City area could now borrow books across multiple systems, and the program partially unified area libraries' electronic catalogs, even across the state line into Kansas. These efforts culminated in the Kansas City Library Consortium in the early 2000s, linking online catalogs and checkouts across multiple metropolitan systems. It was a massive logistical achievement for Bradbury, who was accorded the Ronald G. Bohley Award—for "an individual or individuals whose actions have led libraries to work better together"—by the Missouri Library Association in 2003.

As new locations opened, starting with the Lucile H. Bluford Branch in 1988, the Library implemented fully electronic catalogs accessible through computer termi-nals in each building. That year, Library patrons gained still more options beyond traditional books as collections added comic books to the branches. "We're hoping to attract reluctant readers," librarian Irene Ruiz said. As Associate Director Merrill Toms explained, "We lose a lot of the kids in the teen years." Now, youths could take in the exploits of Wonder Woman, Captain America, and the Fantastic Four or enjoy *fotonovelas*, Spanish-language graphic novel–style books featuring photographs of Mexican celebrities. Bibliographic reference and later multimedia encyclopedias and databases eventually could be accessed via compact disc. Patrons were able to search a growing list of online resources using library computers, and the Library established its own presence on the internet in the mid-1990s.

Easy to overlook amid the wave of technological advances was how the deeper philosophy of librarianship was shifting yet again. Bradbury described this to us as a transformation from an "insular" view, wherein librarians considered themselves just "keepers of the books," to a more welcoming approach that met the community on its own terms. As one example, the Main Library initially lacked public restrooms on the first and second floors while denying upper-level access to anyone without a library card. Presumably these policies were the result of 1950s and '60s design philosophies, meant to reduce the number of patrons lingering without purpose. Among Bradbury's first decisions was to open access to the higher floors and make the building a more comfortable and free space for anyone to spend time.

For these and other efforts, and for the flurry of innovations over the first eight years of his two-decade tenure, in 1991, *Library Journal* named Bradbury the national Librarian of the Year, a remarkable achievement for the system. Bradbury also would increase fundraising from private sources. Nine local business executives helped found the Ewing Kauffman Book Fund with $1.2 million in donations in 1991. Another anonymous donor added $500,000, and the fund augmented book collections on a long-term basis, which was especially important during an era when property tax receipts lagged behind the Library's growing expenses.

The Kauffman Fund was named in honor of Kansas City corporate and civic giant Ewing Marion Kauffman, founder of Marion Laboratories and later owner of baseball's Kansas City Royals. As a young man growing up in the city, he suffered from endocarditis and, while constrained to prolonged bedrest, became a voracious reader of library books, sometimes consuming as many as forty a month. That enthusiasm never waned, and he credited his love of reading for his business success. Kauffman passed away in 1993, but the book fund exists to the present day, confirming a long and productive relationship between the Library and the philanthropic organization he established in 1966, the Ewing Marion Kauffman Foundation.

In the early 1990s, the Library received additional support through a $237,500 challenge grant from the National Endowment for the Humanities. It required the

Library to match three-to-one with private funds, and Bradbury immediately launched a campaign to raise the needed $700,000. The effort was a marked success, and the influx of money allowed the Library to enhance book acquisitions and public programming. During the same period, 1992 to 1993, it secured even more external support from the Missouri State Library to operate the Missouri Statewide Reference Center, a phone service that reached rural residents who lacked adequate library services.

Expanding its funding network, the Library adopted a new collection development policy that resulted in a countervailing trend—the systematic removal of thousands of books from the shelves. Although every public library deaccessions, or "weeds," books from its collection in accordance with circulation policies, the scale of the removals in Kansas City has at times sparked minor public controversy. In 1953, for example, the Library purchased twenty thousand books from the estate of a University of Nebraska professor, Thomas Jefferson Fitzpatrick, for $35,000. By the 1990s, around three thousand of these works belonged to its Fine Arts Collection but were commonly known as the Rare Books Collection. It had great monetary value—some of the volumes dated back hundreds of years—but Bradbury described it as "generally unfocused, basically unused, and largely unattended." He recalled only one occasion when anyone requested one of the books, which at the time were stored on copper-wire bookshelves in the director's office with spillover storage in a nearby conference room and safe.

An internal study of Library collections concluded that while the books sat unused, they did "represent a potentially significant asset which could be converted to cash and otherwise serve the Library's mission." When plans to auction the collection became public, one disapproving Kansas Citian referenced barbarians looting the ancient library of Alexandria, only in this case "it is the librarians themselves who are discarding our literary treasures." The prevailing argument, however, was that other institutions could better preserve the collections, and the constituents of a public library would be better served with proceeds from an auction that exceeded $150,000 in 1994.

Bradbury foresaw a future where, in the face of budget stagnation due to property tax deferrals, the Library would focus less on pushing its physical locations as community centers and more on the development of technology to expand access to its print and digital resources. Books remained crucial to the mission because the printed word created a "sustained narrative," Bradbury noted, whereas "the internet is the 'snack machine for the mind.'" His philosophy looked to thread a needle between expanded collections, technological change, and restricted resources.

Such a plan required compromises, but to Bradbury's and the Library's credit, the circulation of physical materials more than doubled from 1985 to 1995, from 1 million to 2.3 million. A quarter of that increase came from new technologies like videocassettes and compact discs. In the future, Bradbury predicted, buildings would be less architectural marvels and more efficient, pleasant, and businesslike spaces for information delivery. "Now," he said, "you can sit at your home computer or your office computer and plug in to the public library and just access an incredible array of indexes and encyclopedias and databases."

Meanwhile, amid tight finances, the Main Library and Plaza Branch were suffering from the effects of long delays in building maintenance. Downtown, librarians resorted to covering computers in plastic sheets in case water pipes burst without warning. Beyond mechanical issues, the location of the Main Library no longer suited a public library because of a plummeting downtown residential population since the 1960s and an expensive leasing arrangement with the building's owner—still the Kansas City school district. In the Plaza Branch's case, its building was erected on a layer of shale. Because an overlying layer of limestone had been removed, the shale could expand and heave, wrecking the building's foundation within a few years of its opening and leaving no economically feasible path for repair. These situations enmeshed the Library's leadership in a search for new homes.

NEW HOMES:
CENTRAL AND PLAZA LIBRARIES

Today's location of the Central Library was anything but foreseeable to 1990s residents of Kansas City, who had grown accustomed to a downtown devoid of residential spaces, shopping, and nightlife. Words such as "blight," "itinerant," and "vacant" came up frequently in media descriptions of the area. Nor was a downtown location a preferred option for Director Bradbury, who envisioned the Plaza location anchoring a more decentralized branch system. Library trustees and civic leaders had a different vision, however, imagining a downtown Central Library that would spearhead the revitalization of an entire urban district.

Chief among these proponents was J. Philip Kirk Jr., then chair of DST Realty Inc. and an accomplished developer in downtown Kansas City. Kirk's philosophy of urban revitalization translated into a mutually beneficial relationship between private business interests and the Library project: "You couldn't just build buildings. You had to restore the whole social and community fabric." He further reasoned, "We need a place of center where we can rub shoulders with the wisdom and heritage of previous generations, to raise the level of dignity and decency in the world."

Top: Central Library at 14 West Tenth Street, front entrance with fifth-floor addition visible at upper left
Bottom: Kirk Hall, Central Library

While inevitable complications arose in this major civic undertaking, its story appears in hindsight as one of serendipity. The former First National Bank Building at 14 West Tenth Street appeared on the market in 2000, just as Kirk and the Library's board of trustees were searching for a suitable downtown property. Bank of America, the latest in a succession of occupants, had consolidated its offices elsewhere and closed the building, leaving an uncertain fate for the historic structure that had stood since 1906. The neoclassical, marble-appointed building could not feasibly be converted into offices or residential spaces, but with deep investments and vision, its classical features could be preserved while the building was being remade to house a state-of-the-art public library.

The century-old bank building presented an ideal canvas for the architects and civic leaders shaping it into a grand public library. Designed by Edward T. Wilder and Thomas Wight, it had originally opened as the First National Bank on April 15, 1906. First National was a homegrown Kansas City institution founded by James Abernathy and James Lombard in 1886. With marble inside and out, mahogany finishes, bronze entry doors, and six fourteen-ton columns out front, the stately structure projected a sense of permanence and security. A 1925–26 addition added around twenty-eight feet on the east side, followed by a 1968 expansion that added a four-story north wing and two basement levels. The extra space would prove indispensable.

In 1969, First National Bank formed a multibank holding company, and that move was followed by twenty-seven acquisitions over the ensuing decade and a half. The institution became known as CharterCorp, and it opened Kansas City's first ATM in 1976. Later mergers with Boatmen's Bancshares, NationsBank, and Bank of America led to several changes in name and ownership. After the vacated building at Tenth Street and Baltimore Avenue entered the real estate market in 2000, Dan Bradbury described the Library's interest and pursuit as "the convergence of a lot of interests" among Library trustees, the Downtown Council, residents concerned about the fate of a historic structure, and philanthropists.

Other civic leaders and philanthropists joined Kirk in determining the suitability of the downtown bank building. Commerce Bank chairman Jonathan Kemper, Hallmark Foundation vice president John Laney (who chaired the Downtown Council), and Library board president Olivia Dorsey helped spearhead the endeavor and purchased the empty structure for $2 million. Tens of millions more would be needed to restore it and convert it into a public library, but the result, as Kemper described it twenty years later, is a library "built for the ages."

The Downtown Council, a nonprofit organization promoting downtown revitalization, identified nearly $10 million in federal and state historic tax credits that could be applied to the project. The Library would lease the facility initially and buy it from an LLC (formed by the Downtown Council) in 2010. Private foundations, including the William T. Kemper Foundation - Commerce Bank Trustee; Hall Family Foundation; Ewing Marion Kauffman Foundation; Kirk Foundation, Phil and Judy Kirk;

Jonathan Kemper, board of trustees member, former board president, and major donor to the Library

and H&R Block Foundation, provided an additional $25 million through a fund set up by the nonprofit Kansas City Community Foundation.

Vartan Gregorian, then president of the Carnegie Corporation of New York and renowned as the savior of the troubled New York Public Library system in the 1980s, believed that the project would revitalize Kansas City at large. In a keynote address during the public launch of a capital campaign for the new Central Library in October 2002, he predicted "the new library will grace the city, help stimulate a downtown renaissance and—most, most importantly—be better able to play its central role in the cultural, intellectual and democratic life of the entire metropolitan community." His words proved prescient.

Soon after the library project became public knowledge, the dream of downtown revitalization coalesced. Laney noted the emergence of several plans to redevelop office buildings into residential spaces—none of which were under consideration prior to the announcement of the new Central Library, according to Dale Schulte of DLS Real Estate Inc. When completed, several of those buildings were fully leased within three months. With people moving back downtown, opportunities opened for other businesses, such as retail stores, coffee shops, entertainment venues, and restaurants. In turn, still more people moved in.

When the revitalized neighborhood surrounding the Central Library was officially named the Library District in 2003, it cemented the understanding that the
refreshed Library system would be the intellectual and cultural crossroads of Kansas
City. US Representative Emanuel Cleaver II, who has long sponsored the Fifth
District Congressional Art Contest for students at the Central Library, underscored
the importance of the building, saying, "it is a declaration that this community is
alive . . . a downtown without a library is a human without a soul."

In media interviews, Library officials, along with design firm HNTB, invoked the
then-thriving Barnes & Noble bookstores, which drew customers in part by offering
a consistently pleasant and entertaining visitor experience. The earliest renderings
showed an enclosed rooftop winter garden with an arched roof covering as much as
forty thousand square feet. This would have provided visitors a "new, exciting, major
public space that's full of sunlight," as described by HNTB's Richard Farnan. Federal
representatives and historic preservation committees, however, vetoed any rooftop
additions that would alter the street view of the building. The ensuing redesign made
space for a set-back fifth floor, housing the Missouri Valley Room and Gladys Feld
Helzberg Auditorium as well as a rooftop patio and garden space that now hosts
everything from chess games with life-size pieces to movie screenings, yoga sessions,
and an organized viewing in 2017 of a total solar eclipse.

The new Missouri Valley Room added to the grandeur of the building. Its bookshelves, long tucked away in storage, had once graced the 1897 public library on
Locust Street. Stately wood chairs came from Jackson County's local government. The
sliding shelves that to this day house one of Kansas City's most comprehensive archival
collections sat behind glass and were adorned with a massive 1909 photograph of the
block of Baltimore Avenue between Ninth and Tenth Streets. Statues and busts of
prominent regional figures were sprinkled among the chairs, paintings, a grandfather
clock, and lamps that formed a warm, pleasant atmosphere. Many public libraries
had a smattering of historical collections with modest reading rooms accessible by
appointment, but few boasted fully staffed and operational archives such as this.

On the third floor, the Effie Mae Winders Kauffman Grand Reading Room
initially opened as a hybrid traditional reading room and public computer lab, with
around 150 computers spread among tables stretching into the surrounding fourth-
floor mezzanine. In the basement, the old bank vault, with a two-foot-thick, seven-
foot-high, thirty-five-ton door, was preserved and converted into a small movie theater

named for the founder of the locally based AMC Theaters, Stanley H. Durwood. The vault's steel door remains in place, permanently secured in an open position. Just above, a quaint café opened in Kirk Hall to round out the public amenities. The Library also purchased the old Kansas City School of Law building on the Central

Top: Effie Mae Winders Kauffman Grand Reading Room, Central Library
Bottom: Missouri Valley Room and Special Collections, Central Library

Library's north side, converting it into an administrative annex with staff offices, meeting spaces, and a boardroom. In recognition of the renovations and contributions to the rescue of Kansas City's historic downtown, the National Trust recognized the Library with its National Preservation Honor Award.

Next door, across Baltimore Avenue, the Library turned what could have been another nondescript parking garage into a downtown landmark that has received national and even international recognition. The Community Bookshelf, the twenty-eight-foot-tall facade of the parking garage, resembled enormous book spines, each nine feet wide. To create a model, a small group of Library representatives went to the Linda Hall Library of Science and Technology, where they pulled and arranged books to balance the different shapes, designs, and colors of spines. Community surveys guided the Library board's selection of twenty-two titles. Since the moment of the Community Bookshelf's unveiling, awards and acknowledgments have appeared in construction industry publications, library journals, *Popular Mechanics* magazine, travel websites, and other media outlets worldwide.

Early in this transformative period, Dan Bradbury began to think about stepping down from his role as director, allowing new leadership to stabilize revenues, open the new Central Library, and "put their fingerprints on these two big projects and

Community Bookshelf and parking garage, south side, Central Library

get a running start at making them successful." Prior to leaving in January 2003, he ensured that work on the Central Library was on track and negotiated a separate public-private partnership to replace the beleaguered Plaza Branch, which was still dealing with costly structural issues. Transitioning into the new buildings fell to Joseph H. Green, who served as director for a little over a year, followed by interim director Roger Pearson for eight months, and finally Director R. Crosby Kemper III, who served in that capacity from 2005 to early 2020.

The new Plaza Branch would sit in the same location, and once a sentimental "grand closing" ceremony took place, the old building shut down at the end of 2001 to make way for construction. The branch's operations temporarily moved to 301 East Fifty-First Street in a nearby, university-owned building. The temporary site managed with six thousand square feet compared to the previous thirty thousand, but the new branch would encompass fifty thousand square feet and a 350-seat auditorium when completed.

Most inventive—though some critics called it "concerning"—among Bradbury's plans was a financial structure that offered valuable public real estate to private developers in exchange for bearing the burden of building costs. Under the arrangement, the developer Copaken, White & Blitt constructed an eleven-story office building with a two-story retail structure and parking garage. The Library kept ownership of the land, or "footprint," while Copaken and Highwoods Properties obtained a ninety-nine-year lease to manage the property.

At no up-front cost, the Library would receive a "warm building shell" on the main level with a $2.5 million allowance for finishing the space. Crucially, at a time when it was busily fundraising for the Central Library and the system's long-term fiscal sustainability was in doubt, no new taxes or bonds were needed to carry out these plans. Further, by partnering with a private entity, the Library could indirectly leverage the same tax abatements—or tax increment financing—that had long cut into revenues and been what Bradbury called the "bane of our existence." As part of the proposal, the developers would not pay property taxes on the office spaces for twenty-three years, incentivizing construction in the short term and returning the private spaces of the building back to the property tax rolls in the long term.

Despite some remaining rough edges, the grand opening of the new Plaza Branch was a rousing success. "People flooded the building," recalled then manager Joel Jones of the crowd of three thousand that showed up. Now the deputy director of library services, Jones described how eager the public had grown after more than three years of waiting for the new facility. There was free wireless internet. Fifty public computers, while fewer than anticipated, doubled the number at the old branch. At a ribbon cutting the following day, Mayor Kay Barnes boasted, "If our library system is any indication, everything is up to date in Kansas City."

Social scientist Robert Putnam, the author of *Bowling Alone: The Collapse and Revival of American Community*, delivered an opening keynote address and spoke of the Plaza Branch as a powerful symbol of civic renewal. While many questioned the future of libraries in an internet-fueled world, Putnam countered, "Libraries are very far from dead." The Kansas City Public Library had proven that a collective investment in a civic institution could rejuvenate its community. Jones noted that programming for the Plaza Branch's grand opening targeted teenagers with popular games of the day, along with the attractions of online resources, a coffee shop, and a trendy view of the Country Club Plaza. The city's Main MAX bus line connected the branch to points far beyond its immediate neighborhood, and the Plaza became, as Jones described it, "a destination, a meeting space" for the full community.

SIGNATURE PROGRAMMING

The opening of the Central Library and Plaza Branch might have been seen as a culmination of ongoing library development, the next logical stage for a public institution with a long and rich history. Expectations could have focused on the maintenance of routine operations under the constraints of a still-limited annual budget.

As it turned out, however, the achievements of the early 2000s were mere stepping stones toward a flurry of transformations that appear unprecedented in scale since the era of Carrie Westlake Whitney. Library director R. Crosby Kemper III brought a fresh emphasis on public programming, outreach, and digital initiatives, further elevating the Library's standing within the profession and enhancing its reputation with the wider public. While many of these achievements are still fresh in memory and their long-term legacy not yet known, the recent proliferation of innovations has built what appears to be an auspicious foundation for the Library's next 150 years.

The Library's board of trustees had specifically sought a director whose skill set would match the Library's long-term needs and carry the institution in a bold new direction. They grew interested in hiring Crosby Kemper to carry out this vision. Jonathan and Crosby Kemper were second cousins and scions of Kansas City's prominent family of bankers, civic leaders, and philanthropists. Because of the familial ties, Jonathan, who had been elected Library board president in January 2005, recused himself from voting on Crosby's hiring.

The new director started on a temporary basis that same month, and in September the board hired him permanently. In a departure from common industry practice—and state statute—Kemper lacked a master's degree in library science (MLS). For that reason, the Missouri Library Association initially opposed his hiring. What he did bring, per the Library's press release, was deep "financial and marketing expertise" as the former chair and executive director of the UMB Financial Corp., a position he held from 2000 to 2004. By the time of Kemper's hiring at the end of August 2005, he and the board of trustees had successfully lobbied Missouri's legislature to change the law and eliminate the MLS requirement for library directors. Kemper, who admitted to originally viewing the Library as "a quiet and sleepy place," sought to make it one of Kansas City's most important civic forums. In his first three years as director, such advancements became possible as private donations swelled to $5 million, a threefold increase.

The Library's celebrated "signature events" developed when Kemper established the Department of Public Affairs and hired former marketing executive Henry Fortunato as its director in June 2006. He would remain in that position until 2015. Fortunato, according to *The Pitch* magazine's Carolyn Szczepanski, set to work booking speakers "with the zeal of a concert promoter." With his soft-yet-fast speech, eastern manners, suspenders-wearing fashion, thick beard, and penchant for walking long distances (including hiking across Kansas), Fortunato brought an eccentric passion to the position. Kemper relished introducing speakers and serving as the "face" of the library, but so, too, did Fortunato as the number of events exploded from around fifty per year to more than two hundred. The Library went on to host public addresses by such renowned figures as retired US Supreme Court justice Sandra Day O'Connor, women's rights icon Anita Hill, former US secretary of state Condoleezza Rice, and two-time Pulitzer Prize–winning author David McCullough.

Besides Kirk Hall, after April 2008, staff also booked these events in the Truman Forum on the lower level of the Plaza Branch. The Kauffman Foundation provided $2.1 million to complete the auditorium and further expanded its support for public

Retired US Supreme Court justice Sandra Day O'Connor speaking in Kirk Hall, Central Library, June 3, 2013

programming with a $4 million grant, the largest the Library had received to that point. With room to accommodate more than four hundred guests, the Library finally had a welcoming, comfortable public forum with plentiful space for author speaking engagements, receptions, roundtables, and performances on its one-thousand-square-foot stage. "This is where the average citizen can engage with ideas, can engage with public policy, and engage with each other," Kemper said.

Confirmation that something remarkable was happening came in 2008 with the institution's highest level of national recognition to date: its selection for the National Medal for Museum and Library Service from the Institute of Museum and Library Services (IMLS). Presented to Library representatives by First Lady Laura Bush in a ceremony at the White House, the award remains "the nation's highest honor for institutions that make significant and exceptional contributions to their communities."

In addition to broadly sustained excellence, the award nomination cited the Library's Books to Go project, which distributed thousands of books to preschoolers, and other ongoing efforts to bridge cultural and digital divides. The Books to Go program—the largest of its kind in the nation—had been launched by Outreach

Manager Carrie McDonald in 1993 with help from a $36,000 State Library grant. The American Library Association added to the list of Library accolades with its Excellence in Library Programming Award in 2014. Additionally, *Meet the Past with Crosby Kemper III*, a series that appeared on Kansas City PBS, received regional Emmy awards in 2014 and 2015.

Two more awards of note transcended programming. The Library was one of three recipients of the LibraryAware Community Award from *Library Journal* in 2017, recognizing libraries' value to their respective communities. That same year, it was accorded the Humanities Award for Exemplary Community Achievement by the Missouri Humanities Council.

WESTERN FRONTIERS TO DIGITAL FUTURES

In recent years, the Library has increasingly utilized new technologies and policies to engage the widest possible audiences. One example is the Digital Media Lab, which was organized by Crystal Faris, the current deputy director of youth and family engagement. In 2012, Faris secured a MacArthur Foundation grant to support teen education through technology-infused projects and hired Andrea Ellis, who later served as the Library's director of strategic learning, to set up and manage the mobile initiative. The initiative expanded in 2014 with a grant from the Kansas City Digital Inclusion Fund to offer teen programming at neighborhood branches that employed digital cameras, 3D printers, and other technologies.

Coinciding with these efforts, the Library's then deputy director Cheptoo Kositany helped establish the Kansas City Coalition for Digital Inclusion, an independent organization that coordinates the efforts of dozens of companies and nonprofit organizations. Kositany also set up the Digital Branch in 2013. Managed by digital librarian David LaCrone, it offered resources twenty-four hours a day, seven days a week. These ranged from e-books and databases for lifelong learning and research to music and video streaming, news media, content for kids, and job search materials. Combined with print materials, total loans to patrons have since hovered around 2 million items annually.

The Digital Branch has also developed websites directly, utilizing external partnerships and resources from the Missouri Valley Room or other departments.

These efforts have promoted access to partner institutions' collections and deepened the pool of accessible resources for the community to better understand its past and present. Most utilized have been historical websites focused on the Civil War along the Missouri-Kansas border, the 1920s and '30s era in Kansas City, and significant figures in local African American history. Collectively, these sites have won awards from the American Historical Association, the American Association for State and Local History, the Society of Civil War Historians, and the Western History Association.

Carrie Coogan, who became deputy director for public affairs and community engagement in 2015, established the Tech Access initiative with Wendy Pearson, strategic initiatives manager. Their team works closely with external partners, including the federal government's AmeriCorps service agency. With innovative concepts such as the lending of wireless internet hotspots and tablets and direct educational outreach to patrons, it has helped thousands in the community navigate online employment, government, and other services and resources. In 2016, with funding from the William T. Kemper Foundation, the OneNorth Technology Center opened on the main floor of the Central Library, consolidating resources into one space and adding iPads and trained support staff to provide patrons with one-on-one tech consultations.

The Library has adapted to evolving needs and concerns through its Community Reference and Outreach programs in areas including health care, voter information, tax-filing assistance, and support for patrons experiencing homelessness. The new reference model, conceptualized by Joel Jones and implemented by then community reference manager Kim Gile, moved subject experts away from reference desks and out into the community. These specialists are available for one-to-one consultation in small business and entrepreneurship, health and wellness, legal and government information, and career development and personal finance.

Similarly, as the Library sought to enhance social services supporting the needs of patrons experiencing homelessness, Mary Olive Joyce, the Library's current director of library outreach and community engagement, established the Community Resources department. These outreach efforts consolidated and expanded the Library's programs to better connect patrons to social service providers across the city.

In years when funding has been secured from the National Endowment for the Arts and Arts Midwest, Director of Readers' Services Kaite Stover organizes The Big Read, an initiative that centers a series of public programs on a particular literary work and theme. Each year, Stover, along with Crystal Faris and many others across the Library system, implements Summer Reading programs to promote youth and adult readership. Patrons in need can turn to the Library for assistance in completing forms for utilities, rent, and housing; for locating free meals, food pantries, clothing, and showers; and for finding medical and dental care.

Ever since the widespread adoption of broadcast radio and automobiles in the early twentieth century, the Kansas City Public Library has embraced new concepts in technology, architecture, outreach, and programming to serve the diverse interests of the people of Kansas City and beyond. Library employees routinely extend these services outside the walls of the Library and the boundaries of Kansas City, reflected in the 2023 election of the Library's director of policy analysis and operational support Cindy Hohl as president-elect of the American Library Association.

Today, the Library continues to promote an understanding of learning that begins with literacy yet extends far beyond that to provide a diverse educational experience that enriches and empowers its patrons and community. Its many innovations in librarianship advance information literacy, opportunity, and critical thinking— all paramount in the stubbornly complicated and technological world of the twenty-first century.

INTO THE NEXT CENTURY

*The Kansas City Public Library is a focal point of intellectual
conversation in our community . . . it houses the freedom of opportunity
which our nation cherishes as the cornerstone of its efficacy.*
—CONGRESSMAN EMANUEL CLEAVER II

T he growth of the Library system, especially the expansion of its celebrated public outreach, signature events, and digital services, underscored the need for additional financial resources to sustain this success for the long term. In the second decade of the twenty-first century, revenue from a property tax levy that accounts for 90 percent of the Library's budget grew by less than 1 percent annually. The Library was operating in 2018 under a levy appropriation set in 1996. Yet demand for services expanded precipitously over that time, evidenced by the more than four million patrons who visited in 2017 and 2018 alone. The Library needed additional revenue to continue this high level of community engagement.

The Library took its case to the people of Kansas City and Jackson County, seeking an eight-cent increase in the levy—the first adjustment in twenty-two years. "More than ever," its website announced, the Kansas City Public Library "is central to the lives of the individuals, families, and communities it serves. From early childhood literacy to outreach for the elderly and disabled. From access to computers and the internet to civic and community engagement." By any measure, the Library had successfully integrated into the community's social fabric and become one of its most indispensable institutions.

Top: The Library's new Bookmobile, 2020

Bottom: R. Crosby Kemper III speaking in Kirk Hall, September 29, 2018

Voters signaled their agreement in November 2018, giving the measure 83 percent approval. It was a stunning margin, one of the largest—if not *the* largest—for a library ballot measure anywhere in the nation, testifying to the unique social capital the Library had built over a century and a half.

Additional revenues from the levy increase have permitted the Library to not just sustain current operations but also expand its programming, services, and renovations. Moreover, it emphasized equal access. This philosophy manifested in June 2019 as the Library implemented a new Freedom from Fines policy, becoming one of the nation's first public systems to permanently eliminate late fees in book lending. The measure immediately canceled $250,000 of uncollected fines. The American Library Association had identified fines as a form of "social inequity" that presented barriers to access for lower-income patrons, especially for children and youth, and many libraries across the country have since followed the example set in Kansas City.

With expanded revenue, the Library finally could address long-deferred maintenance on roofs, air conditioners, and restrooms. Staffing levels recovered after decreasing by 7.5 percent over the previous decade, allowing the system to restore operating hours and capacity for services. Major renovations were completed at the North-East Branch and physical needs identified at the Waldo and Bluford branches to be addressed. New outreach, education, and advocacy efforts started through the Refugee & Immigrant Services & Empowerment (RISE) program. Public computers could be replaced, and new ones added. Outreach further expanded with a reconstituted Bookmobile, four additional vehicles, and an upgraded Mobile Device Lab. Tellingly, Library leadership and employees accomplished much of this amid the backdrop of the COVID-19 pandemic.

The RISE initiative is especially important as Kansas City's immigrant population continues to grow. The Kansas City Public Library became one of the first public libraries in the United States to devote a full-time manager to serving refugee and immigrant populations when it appointed Julie Robinson to oversee the initiative in September 2014. It offers a range of services, including English Language Learning (ELL) courses and preparation for naturalization. The US District Court for the Western District of Missouri has made the Central Library a frequent location for naturalization ceremonies since 2016.

Perhaps it was inevitable that Director Crosby Kemper would be called to higher service. He received and accepted a presidential nomination in 2019 to lead the

Institute of Museums and Library Services, the independent federal agency that eleven years earlier had honored the Library with the National Medal. Upon his departure from the Library in January 2020, Assistant Director Debbie Siragusa served as interim director through spring 2020, guiding the institution through the early stages of COVID-19—one of the most unnerving, uncertain, and strenuous times in its long history. That summer, the Library hired Executive Director John Herron, formerly interim dean of UMKC's College of Arts and Sciences, to see the Library through the pandemic and into a new era.

Bestowal of the National Medal in 2008 best affirmed, and still sums up, what the people of Kansas City already know and continue to express: The Kansas City Public Library is an indispensable cultural and intellectual hub, a powerful center of public service. Representative Emanuel Cleaver II, who originally nominated the Library for the honor, elaborated in a speech to the US House that his hometown Library "allows our citizenry to explore its role as America's heartland, evolving from a frontier city to a modern-day metropolis with racial and cultural diversity."

Cleaver described the Library as "a focal point of intellectual conversation in our community," and indeed, in contemporary Kansas City, that is exactly what it has become. Beyond noting the robust portfolio of services and programs, Cleaver paid tribute to an institution that "houses the freedom of opportunity which our nation cherishes as the cornerstone of its efficacy." Our Library, he concluded, has "played a role in almost every social movement" in Kansas City's history. He pointed to Alvin Sykes and his work for racial justice—forever linked to the Library—as evidence of the Library's capacity to empower its community for the betterment of all. With such an extraordinary record and the unremitting support of its patrons, the Kansas City Public Library is prepared to make the next 150 years as distinguished as the first.

BIBLIOGRAPHY

SPECIAL COLLECTIONS SOURCES

American Civil Liberties Union Records. MC#001 box 785, folder 18, Kansas City, MO: Police Confiscation, 1957–1959.

American Library Association vertical file, SC63. Missouri Valley Special Collections (MVSC), Kansas City Public Library, Kansas City, Missouri.

"Annual Report of the Kansas City Public Library, 1917–1918." MVSC.

Barbara [name hidden in original for privacy] to Phyllis Lyon, November 12, 1964. Daughters of Bilitis collection, box 6, folder 9. Gay, Lesbian, Bisexual, and Transgender Historical Society, Archives of Sexuality and Gender. Gale Primary Sources.

Bishop, Frances. Burial records, block 37, lot 103, spaces 2 and 3, Forest Hill Calvary Cemetery, Kansas City, Missouri.

Bradbury, Daniel, et al. "The Cost of Progress: Financial Analysis of the Kansas City Public Library Branch Study—1984." MVSC.

Bradbury, Daniel, et al. "Kansas City Public Library Branch Study: 1984: The Report of the Branch Study Task Force." December 1984. MVSC.

Cherry, Susan Spaeth. "Public Library Branches in Schools: The Kansas City Experience." *American Libraries* 13, no. 1, 75th Anniversary Issue (January 1982): 24–25, 27–28. MVSC.

Christian, Shirley. "Carrie Westlake Whitney," transcript from lecture delivered at the Kansas City Public Library, May 26, 2010. Vertical file, SC63. MVSC.

Cleaver, Emanuel, II. "Recognizing the Outstanding Achievements of the Kansas City Public Library." *U.S. Congressional Record* 155, no. 56 (April 2, 2009): E862.

Community Studies Inc. *Community Studies Review.* MVSC.

Community Studies Inc. "A Study of Branch Library Location and Service: Kansas City, Missouri." December 1952. MVSC.

Compton, Charles H. "Missouri's New Constitution and the Free Public Library." *Library Journal* 70, no. 19 (November 1, 1945): 1001–1003. MVSC.

Faxon, Frank A. to Purd B. Wright, telegram. January 13, 1911. MVSC.

Fuhri, Ursula Fiona. "History of the Lincoln Branch." Handwritten manuscript. MVSC.

Goldsmith, Katherine. "Approaching Kansas City: From All Points of the Compass." *American Library Association Bulletin* 62, no. 5 (May 1968): 531–34. Magazine Article Photocopies, SC73. MVSC.

Greenlee, John Rankin. "Kansas City Public Library World War II Honor Book, 1939-1946." Kansas City Public Library Collection, SC6. MVSC.

Greenwood, James M. *A History of the Kansas City Public Library: From 1873 to 1893.* Kansas City, MO: Rigby-Ramsey Printing Co., 1893. MVSC.

Gregorian, Vartan. "Libraries as Acts of Civic Renewal." Transcript from lecture delivered at the Kansas City Club. October 17, 2002. MVSC.

Grier, Barbara. Tape 7. Interview includes segment with Donna McBride, Lesbian Herstory Archives AudioVisual Collections. November 27, 1987. Audio, 01:53:02. http://herstories.prattinfoschool.nyc/omeka/items/show/400.

Guadalupe Center Collection, SC20, MVSC.

Hispanic Oral History Collection, SC69-1. MVSC.

"History Unfolds in Downtown Library." *Northeast World* 1, no. 26 (December 10, 1986). MVSC.

Kansas City Chapter of the American Institute of Architects. *Skylines* (December 1960). MVSC.

Kansas City Public Library. "Eightieth Anniversary Report: Your Library Looks Ahead, 1874–1954." MVSC.

Kansas City Public Library. "Kansas City Public Library: Our History in Words & Pictures." MVSC.

Kansas City Public Library. "KCPL: 25 Years at 311 E. 12th Street, 1985." MVSC.

Kansas City Public Library. "Library's New Home Offers Wealth of History," March/April 2004 Calendar. MVSC.

Kansas City Public Library. *Library Staff News* 22, no. 3 (September 1943). MVSC.

Kansas City Public Library. *Library Staff News* 51, no. 2 (June-July 1973). MVSC.

Kansas City Public Library. "Murals in the Library." MVSC.

Kansas City Public Library and KCMO Radio. Radio Scripts, Volumes 1 and 2, 1944–1946. MVSC.

Kansas City Public Library Scrapbooks, 1915–1999, SC30-4. MVSC.

Katherine Goldsmith Papers, RH MS 1093. Kenneth Spencer Research Library, University of Kansas, Lawrence, Kansas.

Kemper, Jonathan. "Remarks to the Kansas City Tomorrow Class." Central Library, September 17, 2010. MVSC.

Kinney, Marjorie. "The Missouri Valley Room of the Kansas City Public Library." *Show-Me Libraries* 24, no. 8 (Missouri State Library, May 1973). MVSC.

Kirk, Stephen, and Emanuel Cleaver II, Correspondence. June 8–16, 1972. MVSC.

Lenrow, Michael S., and Gary S. Sasse. "Libraries in Metropolis: A Study of Public Library Services in the Kansas City and St. Louis Metropolitan Areas." (Kansas City, MO: Community Studies, 1966). MVSC.

"Librarian's Report[s]." Various. MVSC.

Libraries: Kansas City Public: 9th and Locust. Vertical file, SC63. MVSC.

Libraries: Kansas City Public: 12th and Oak, 1 and 2. Vertical files, SC63. MVSC.

Libraries: Kansas City Public: Central (10th and Baltimore). Vertical file, SC63. MVSC.

Libraries: Kansas City Public: Friends of the Library. Vertical file, SC63. MVSC.

Libraries: Kansas City Public: Missouri Valley Room. Vertical file, SC63. MVSC.

Libraries: Kansas City Public: Plaza Branch. Vertical file, SC63. MVSC.

Libraries: Kansas City Public. Vertical files on branches, SC63. MVSC.

Lincoln Collection. Black Studies Research Center, Ramos Special Collection. MVSC.

Lincolnite. Yearbooks from Lincoln High School. MVSC.

Matthews, Bruce. "Getting It Right: The History of the Kansas City Public Library." Unpublished manuscript. MVSC.

Missouri v. Jenkins—515 U.S. 70. Law School Case Brief. LexisNexis. https://www.lexisnexis.com/community/casebrief/p/casebrief-missouri-v-jenkins.

"Mrs. Carrie Westlake Whitney." November 30, 1895. MVSC.

"MVR: The Dedication of the Missouri Valley Room." Program, Central Library. September 16, 2004. MVSC.

National Register of Historic Places Inventory Nomination Form: Kansas City Public Library and US Trade Schools Inc. (500 East 9th Street). US Department of the Interior, National Park Service, 1976. https://mostateparks.com/sites/mostateparks/files/KC%20Public%20Library.pdf.

National Register of Historic Places Inventory Nomination Form: West Ninth Street/Baltimore Avenue Historic District. https://mostateparks.com/sites/mostateparks/files/W%209th%20St-Baltimore%20Ave%20HD%20BI.pdf.

National Register of Historic Places Registration Form: Kansas City Public Library and Board of Education Building (1211 McGee Street). US Department of the Interior, National Park Service, May 15, 2017. https://mostateparks.com/sites/mostateparks/files/KC%20Public%20Library%20and%20Board%20of%20Education%20Bldg.pdf.

Nistendirk, Verna. "Survey of the Kansas City (Mo.) Public Library: Branches and Extension Agencies." (Kansas City, MO: Kansas City Public Library, 1943). MVSC.

The Phoenix Newsletter. Gay and Lesbian Archives of Mid-America, LaBudde Special Collections, University of Missouri-Kansas City.

Schirmer, Sherry Lamb. *Historical Overview of the Ethnic Communities in Kansas City.* (Kansas City, MO: Pan-Educational Institute, 1976). MVSC.

Sealock, Richard B. "Capital Outlay Needs: Buildings—Equipment—Grounds of the Public Library, Kansas City, Missouri: A Report." (January 30, 1956). MVSC.

Severance, Henry O. *Missouri in the Library War Service.* The University of Missouri Bulletin, July 1931. MVSC.

Shores, Louis. "Public Services to Negroes: Existing Facilities for Training the Negro Compiled from Questionnaires Sent to Librarians of Over Eighty Cities." *Library Journal* (February 15, 1930): 150–54. Interlibrary Loan at Whitworth University Library, Spokane, WA.

"Statement from the Board of Trustees of the Kansas City Public Library: New Plaza Library on Track; Plans Scaled Down." (June 15, 2004). Plaza branch files, Joel Jones, Kansas City Public Library.

Suttell, Robin. "Book Smarts: Grand Prize Winner: Kansas City Downtown Public Library, Kansas City, MO." Buildings.com (June 2005). MVSC.

Sykes, Alvin. "A Conversation with Alvin Sykes." January 30, 2014. Signature Event Archive, Kansas City Public Library, Internet Archive. https://archive.org/details/2014130AlvinSykes.

Turner, Duane, et al. "Public Library Service in Missouri: A Survey." (Missouri State Library, 1962).

US Census Records.

"Walt Disney Letter." August 17, 1937. Henry R. Rule Autograph Collection, SC35-2. MVSC.

Western Gallery of Art. Vertical file, SC63. MVSC.

"We Were There: A New Chapter for Downtown." The Community Foundation. MVSC.

Wheeler, Joseph L. "Report of a Survey of Kansas City Public Library Building Problems, January 28–February 7, 1947." (Kansas City, MO: Kansas City Public Library, 1947). MVSC.

White, William Allen to Purd B. Wright, Correspondence, November 6, 1924. William Allen White vertical file, SC63. MVSC.

Whitney, Carrie Westlake. "K.C., The Library." MVSC.

Williams, Henry Sullivan. "The Development of the Negro Public School System in Missouri: The Period from 1865 to 1875." *The Journal of Negro History* 5, no. 2 (April 1920): 137–65. SC73: Collection of Magazine Article Photocopies. MVSC.

Wright, Purd B. Vertical file, SC63. MVSC.

INTERVIEWS

Arney, Mary, with Steve Wieberg. April 2023.

Bradbury, Daniel J. May 25, 2022, and June 15, 2022.

Cleaver, Emanuel, II. September 1, 2022.

Faris, Crystal, with Steve Wieberg. April 2023.

Jackson-Leathers, Gloria, with Anne Kniggendorf. April 10, 2023.

Jones, Joel. August 18, 2022.

Kemper, Jonathan. September 6, 2022.

NEWSPAPERS

The Call (Kansas City)

The Kansas City Journal

The Kansas City Star

The Kansas City Sun
The Kansas City Times
The Martin City Telegraph
The New York Times
The Pitch Weekly
The Rising Son (Kansas City)
Show-Me Libraries
St. Louis Post-Dispatch

JOURNALS

The Indian School Journal
Kansas City Magazine
The Kansas City Public Library Quarterly
Library Journal
Missouri History Encyclopedia
Missouri Library Association Handbook, 1915
Missouri Library World
The Negro History Bulletin
Westport Magazine
Wilson Bulletin for Librarians

PUBLISHED WORKS

Amick, Jeremy. "'The Call of Missouri,' WWI Painting by Renowned Muralist Vanished from Original Kansas City Home." *California Democrat* (April 9, 2017).

Bradbury, Daniel J. "Barbarians within the Gate: Pillage of a Rare Book Collection?" *Rare Books & Manuscripts Librarianship* 9, no. 1 (1994): 8–16.

Buckley, Michelle. "Former Bank of America Building Becomes Library's New Home." *The Business Journal: Serving Metropolitan Kansas City* 19, no. 14 (December 15, 2000): 32.

Cashill, Jack. "How the Public Library Transformed Kansas City." *Ingram's* (March 2011). https://ingrams.com/archive/Mar_2011/ImagesandArticles/BetweentheLines/btl.html.

Chamber of Commerce of Kansas City. "Nation's Most Popular Library." *The Kansas Citian: A Journal Issued on Behalf of the Business and Civic Interests of Kansas City* (August 1944): 7, 33.

Chen, Jen. "From Banking to Books: The KC Public Library's Crosby Kemper III." Central Standard, KCUR 89.3. (August 3, 2016). https://www.kcur.org/show/central-standard/2016-08-03/from-banking-to-books-the-kc-public-librarys-crosby-kemper-iii.

Conard, Howard L. *Encyclopedia of the History of Missouri, A Compendium of History and Biography for Ready Reference. Vols. I–VI.* New York: Haldeman, Conard, and Co., 1901.

Davis, Jim. "Kirk Serves as Quiet Architect of Downtown's Rebirth." *Kansas City Business Journal* 25, no. 43 (June 29, 2007): 10.

Dodd, Monroe. "Pursuit of Truth: From Kansas City's Libraries, Alvin Sykes Plotted an Unlikely Course to Civil Rights History." Kansas City Public Library (January 2014). https://kclibrary.org/sites/default/files/Alvin%20Sykes%20-%20Pursuit%20of%20Truth.pdf.

"Edwin Howland Blashfield (1848-1936): Trumpets of Missouri," Christie's Auctions, May 21, 2014. https://www.christies.com/en/lot/lot-5793659.

Ewing Marion Kauffman Foundation. "Celebrate the Legacy: Ewing Kauffman's Life Took Him on an Unconventional Path that Allowed him to Enrich the Lives of Others Along the Way." https://www.kauffman.org/emk/.

"Excellence in Development Award—Plaza Colonnade." *Kansas City Business Journal* (November 17–23, 2006).

"Films Aid Popularity of Books." *The Moving Picture World* (July 7, 1917): 88.

"FrontDesk: No MLS for Interim Head in Kansas City." *Library Journal* (February 15, 2005).

Garrison, Dale. "KC Library: The (Re-)Making of a Legend." *Ingram's* (February 2004).

Greenwood, James M. *A History of the Kansas City Public Library From 1873 to 1893.* Kansas City, MO: Rigby-Ramsey Printing Co., 1893.

"Has Financial Independence." *Library Journal* 71, no. 8 (October 15, 1946): 1438.

Hoffman, William H. *Kansas City Missouri Public Library, 1873-1973: An Illustrated History.* Kansas City, MO: Kansas City Public Library, 1973.

Hyers, Faith Holmes. "Radio Broadcasting Round Table. Proceedings of the Annual Conference." *Bulletin of the American Library Association* 31, no. 11 (October 15, 1937): 804–8.

Jennings, Kathryn Lynn. *Kansas City Public Library and the School System, 1873 to 1898.* Columbia: University of Missouri Press, 1971.

"The Kansas City Public Library." *The City Ice Man* 1, no. 7 (Kansas City, MO: September 1924).

Kansas City Public Library. "Freedom from Fines." https://kclibrary.org/finefree.

Kansas City Public Library. "Remembering Alvin Sykes: A 'Dogged, Deeply Infused Passion.'" (March 19, 2021). https://kclibrary.org/blog/remembering-alvin-sykes-%E2%80%98dogged-deeply-infused-passion%E2%80%99.

Kansas City Public Library. "Thank You, Voters!" (2018). https://kclibrary.org/election.

Kavanaugh, Lee Hill. "Long Lost Art is Found." *The Hawk Eye* (May 27, 2013).

Kiliper, Lindsay. "Literary Deposits." *KC Chronicle* (March 2004).

"The Library and the Returning Veteran." *Library Journal* 70, no. 7 (April 1, 1945): 293–96.

"'The Library Saved My Life': LGBTQ Books 2017." *Publishers Weekly* 264, no. 22 (May 26, 2017): 43.

Magerl, Barbara. "Atkins, Mary, Benefactress, 1836–1911." Biographical sketch, MVSC. https://kchistory.org/document/biography-mary-atkins-1836-1911-benefactress.

Mason, Randy. "A Lifeline for Ideas." *KC Studio* (April 26, 2019). https://kcstudio.org/lifeline-for-ideas-kansas-city-public-library/.

McFadden, Robert D. "Vartan Gregorian, Savior of the New York Public Library, Dies at 87." *New York Times.* (April 16, 2021).

"Missouri." *Library Journal* 71, no. 22 (December 15, 1946): 1801–1802.

Nourse, Louis M. "A Constitutional Victory." *ALA Bulletin* 39, no. 6 (June 1945): 201–4.

Peet, Lisa. "Two Kansas City Libraries Defend Free Speech: Patron, Librarian Arrested; Display Title Challenged." *Library Journal* 141, no. 18 (November 1, 2016): 14–15.

Perez, Suzanne. "More and More Kansas Libraries Are Fine with You Not Paying Overdue Fees." KMUW, KCUR 89.3 (March 20, 2022). https://www.kcur.org/news/2022-03-20/more-and-more-kansas-libraries-are-fine-with-you-not-paying-overdue-fees.

Raletz, Alyson. "Google Study Computes the Digital Divide in Kansas City." *Kansas City Business Journal* (June 29, 2012).

Rodriguez, Lisa. "For the First Time in 22 Years, the Kansas City Public Library is Asking for Taxpayers' Help." KCUR Public Radio (October 9, 2018). https://www.kcur.org/politics-elections-and-government/2018-10-09/for-the-first-time-in-22-years-the-kansas-city-public-library-is-asking-for-taxpayers-help.

Ruiz, Vicki L., and Virginia Sanchez Korrol, eds. *Latinas in the United States: A Historical Encyclopedia, Volume I.* Bloomington: Indiana University Press, 2006, 649–50.

Shipman, Joseph C. "Linda Hall Library: 5109 Cherry Street, Kansas City, Missouri." *Library Journal* 71, no. 20 (November 15, 1946): 1587–90.

Stauffer, Suzanne M. "Let Us Forget This Cherishing of Women in Library Work: Women in the American Library War Service, 1918–1920." *Libraries: Culture, History, and Society* 3, no. 2 (2019): 155–74.

Stiles, T. J. *Jesse James: Last Rebel of the Civil War.* New York: Vintage Books, 2003.

Szczepanski, Carolyn. "Life of Kemper." *The Pitch: Kansas City's Independent Source for News and Culture* (November 13, 2008). https://www.thepitchkc.com/life-of-kemper/.

Watson, Paula D. "Founding Mothers: The Contribution of Women's Organizations to Public Library Development in the United States." *The Library Quarterly: Information, Community, Policy* 64, no. 3 (July 1994): 233–69.

Whitney, Carrie Westlake. *Kansas City, Missouri: Its History and Its People, 1800-1908, Volumes I-III.* Chicago: S. J. Clarke Publishing Co., 1908.

Wieberg, Steve. "What To Do With That Old Bank Vault in the Basement?" *KC Studio: Covering Kansas City's Performing, Visual, Cinematic and Literary Arts* (January 18, 2016).

Wiegand, Wayne A. *Part of Our Lives: A People's History of the American Public Library.* New York: Oxford University Press, 2015.

"With New Facility and Greater Space, Plaza Library Services and Staff Will Expand to Meet Many Needs." *Westport/Midtown Back Pages* (March 2005).

Wright, Purd. *Historical Sketch of the Kansas City Public Library, 1911–1936: With Extracts from Annual Reports of Librarian, 1911–1920.* Kansas City, MO: The School District of Kansas City, 1937.

Wright, Purd. "Public Library Established in 1873." *Kansas Citian* (September 10, 1929): 39, 83.

Ziegler, Laura. "Alvin Sykes, Self-Taught Legal Scholar and Civil Rights Advocate, Dies at 64." KCUR Public Radio (March 19, 2021). https://www.kcur.org/news/2021-03-19/alvin-sykes-self-taught-legal-scholar-and-civil-rights-advocate-dies-at-64.

DISSERTATIONS AND THESES

Fuhri, Ursula Fiona. "A History of Services to Black People by the Kansas City, Missouri Public Library." April 1978. MA Thesis, University of Missouri-Columbia.

Love, William N. "A Compilation of Research Concerning Some of the Problems Facing the Kansas City, Missouri School District." May 1977. EdD Dissertation, University of Kansas, Lawrence, Kansas.

Poos, Bradley W. "Desegregation at Kansas City's Central High School: Illuminating the African American Student Experience Through Oral History." 2014. PhD Dissertation, University of Missouri-Kansas City. https://mospace.umsystem.edu/xmlui/handle/10355/43502.

Thomas, Annette Wiehl. "The Kansas City Public Library, 1897-1960: An Architectural Icon." 1997. MA Thesis, Wichita State University.

Wiberg, Ella Lydia. "The History of the Development of Public Education in Kansas City, Missouri." 1925. MA Thesis, University of Wisconsin.

IMAGE CREDITS

Unless otherwise noted: Missouri Valley Special Collections or Public Affairs departments, Kansas City Public Library.

Book Cover: Mike Sinclair, 2008.

Chapter Two: World War I poster showing the Statue of Liberty in ruins. Library of Congress Prints and Photographs Division, Washington, DC.

Chapter Three: Map of public library districts in the Kansas City metropolitan area. Community Studies Inc., "Libraries in Metropolis."

Chapter Five: Images of the Central Library at 14 West Tenth Street, Street, including the front entrance, Kirk Hall, Kauffman Grand Reading Room, Missouri Valley Room, and Community Bookshelf. Courtesy of Bruce Matthews. Photo of Jonathan Kemper, Tiffany Matson Photography.